Trapped

In a Little Girl's Body

A true story of abuse, molestation, forgiveness and triumph

*The
Autobiography of
Los Angeles Publicist &
Concert Promoter*

Dorean
Edwards

Dorean's book is a must read! It tells the story of a strong, courageous woman who survived an unbelievable life, through her faith in God and herself. I am in awe of her!

Barbara Wilson, Producer of The Stellar Awards

No matter how hard the trials and tribulation you faced in life, God had a purpose. Most times we don't understand, but He never left you alone. He covered you with grace and mercy and prepared you, for who you have become today. The late, great *Douglas Miller* once said, "My soul is anchored in the Lord." God is your anchor.

Gerald Alston
R&B Grammy Legend & Lead Singer of The Manhattans

Dorean has captured the essence of the height, depth, length and breadth of God's love and mercy in the writing of this book. The book will help others transitioning from the shadows of pain and abuse, but have not yet overcome the stigma of a lost identity, due to the pain. The conscience decision Dorean made to forgive her perpetrators afforded her the freedom to move forward in life to become the person God created her to be. This book will help you realize the inherent potential that God has invested in you, to become 'More Than a Conqueror.'

Bishop Noel Jones, City of Refuge Church

Dedication

This book is dedicated first and foremost
To my Lord and Savior, Jesus Christ;
And to my mother, Bernadean Edwards Clemons
And my dad, Johnny Lee Edwards

And to all my readers who feel abandoned
Hurt, misused or rejected
Which can lead to low self-esteem

Introduction

I, Dorean Edwards, wrote this book *Trapped in a Little Girl's Body* to encourage anyone that has ever been abused, that they can overcome hurt, be healed and delivered. It was not an easy emotional journey, but I've learned that through the love of God all things are possible. Then again, life is all about a journey, from birth unto death. My journey comes from abuse, shame and hiding -- to deliverance.

I will continue my journey in life sharing with others of how God delivered me and how forgiveness changed my life. I found myself living my life as a reflection of hurt, neglect. I was emotionally crippled until it stripped my self-esteem down to almost nothing.

I was trapped in a little girl's body until I refused to let my past circumstances hold me in bondage. God created me to be free and when I forgave others and myself, I was able to move forward and receive the blessings God had for me. Now I am confident to say, I have conquered my fears and through God I am able to share with you my life experiences. My prayer is that you will learn how to forgive others as I did.

Oftentimes, we silence ourselves with the fear of hurting someone else, even those that hurt us. We do not know what triggers a person to act negatively towards someone else. Money can provide you many things but it cannot buy happiness; it cannot buy love.

I'm wiping the last tear rolling down my face as I remember my past and replaced those tears with a smile. I now embrace each day with love, peace and a humble spirit and I hope you will do the same.

As long as you have God in your life and put him first, you will be on the path of healing and deliverance. God makes no mistakes. Stop blaming yourself for being the victim of someone's actions towards you. Today is a new chapter of your life and a new you.

Dorean Edwards

Table of Contents

What happens when a parent is several
nightmares removed from the ideal?

"Woe unto him who commits offenses!
It would be better for him that
A millstone were hung around his neck
And he be thrown into the ocean
Than offend one of these little ones."

Christ, Luke 17: 1 & 2

Paradise

I took the gun and pressed it against my head. At that moment, the gun became my way out. I was enraptured by its cold, glistening metal and felt its surge of power in my hand. For me, death was paradise. The gun whispered freedom to me; freedom from pain, humiliation and suffering.

Life had stripped me of all self-worth. I felt like a parasite swimming aimlessly in the cesspool of non-existence. I began to question why I was given this gun. It was as though fate met me on the street and invited me to shoot myself. With all my friends looking on in horror, why not go out with a bang.

"Hey look at me, everyone! I'm gonna' kill myself!"

The year was 1969 and I was sixteen years old. Several, significant events occurred that year, including my imminent suicide attempt.

Richard Nixon was inaugurated as the 37th President of the United States. The Apollo 11 astronauts, Neil Armstrong and Edwin Aldrin, Jr., became the first humans to walk on the moon.

1969 was also the year of *Woodstock*, where more than half a million young people gathered for a three-day music festival in upstate New York, featuring the now legendary performances of *Jimi Hendrix, Sly & the Family Stone* and *Janice Joplin.*

Diana Ross, Marvin Gaye and the *Isley Brothers* topped the R&B charts that year, while *Joe Jackson* parted ways with *Steeltown Records* and signed *The Jackson 5* with *Motown.* Meantime, a *Rolling Stones* fan was killed at their Altamont, California, concert, by members of the *Hell's Angels* biker gang. Furthermore, college campuses all over America erupted in protests against the war in Viet Nam; a war into which world-champion, professional boxer, Cassius Clay, refused to be drafted. But none of those events meant a thing to me. I had my own wars to fight right there in my bedroom.

One fine day in the spring of 1969, my mother sent me to the store to buy her a pack of cigarettes. We lived on Ewing Street in a suburb of St. Louis, Missouri. A few blocks down the street from our house stood a neighborhood grocery store with a unique floorplan; groceries on one side, and a sort of 1950s soda-shop on the other. It was here where teenagers gathered from all over the neighborhood after school, to dance and listen to the latest hits on the jukebox.

Along the way to the store, I ran into one of my brothers. Walking up to me, he reached into his pocket and covertly handed me a gun. He asked me to take it home and tell no one about it. I looked at the gun in my hand, completely unafraid, and asked him if there were any bullets in it, and he said there were not. Then he walked away.

I was dazzled by the gun. Its cold, smooth barrel sang to me. Dangerous thoughts flashed through my mind then. *Why not take the pistol and shoot myself in the head? If I do kill myself, no one would miss me, anyway.* It didn't matter to anyone whether I lived or died. The gleam of the gun sent me to a soothing, restful place; a cool meadow far away from there. It seemed to know that

I had recently become suicidal. So I walked into the teen hang-out and looked around a few seconds. Just then, *It's Your Thing* by the *Isley Brothers* played on the juke-box ... *It's your thing ... do what you wanna' do ... I can't tell ya' ... who to sock it to.* How appropriate. So I took the gun and pressed it against my head.

"Hey look at me, everyone! I'm gonna' kill myself!"

Everyone in the shop stopped what they were doing. The kids outside saw it too and stood frozen, looking in. Some of them ran outside, horrified. Once it became apparent that I meant business, a collective hush fell over the crowd as all eyes were on me.

"Dorean, what are you doing?" someone called out.

"Put the gun down, Dorean!" called another.

"Don't shoot yourself!"

"Why do you want to kill yourself?!"

I snapped out of it once I heard the shouting, but I wasn't embarrassed in the slightest. I was done hiding the shame of my existence and done hiding the things that were happening to me at home. By then the pain of abuse I'd suffered in the past decade far out-weighed the spectacle I now created on the street. So there I stood. To me it seemed like a good day to stage my own death. As the cold metal of the barrel pressed against my head, paradise beckoned me and I was about to pull the trigger; if only for special effects, since there weren't any bullets in it – or so I thought. Then I spilled my guts out to the crowd.

"I'm gonna' kill myself!" I screamed with tears streaming down my face. Years of oppressed rage and suffering spilled out of me then, in rapid, one-two-three succession. If I couldn't get attention at home, I'd get it on the street. So I enlisted the crowd into public service; that of my own suicide watch. "No one loves me!" I screamed again.

A decade of psychological strain got the better of me that day, and now I wanted to hurt others as I had been hurt. So without further ado, I brandished the gun at the crowd, whereupon they all ran away. Too bad, really. Someone had finally started listening to me.

Someone ran to tell my brother, so I threw the gun under a chair inside the shop. And then, inexplicably, I went into the grocery section and bought cigarettes for my mother. Just then my brother ran up.

"Where's the gun!" he spat in hushed tones, "Dorean, where's the gun?"

"Right there," and I pointed to the chair.

"Girl, don't you know that you can go to jail carrying this gun?" he said, quickly stuffing it into his pants. "Someone could have called the police on you."

That's when he told me there actually was a bullet in the gun, and then he walked away. Now, here comes our mother scurrying up the street toward me; her steps irate and her face fierce. She was unaware of what I had just done and was furious that I hadn't returned with her cigarettes.

Once my mother arrived at my spot she shouted, "What took you so long?!" Then she slapped the cigarettes out of my hand and knocked me to the ground, right there on the street, in front of my peers.

Death was paradise to me and I wanted to die. Humiliation now flushed over my face as I saw, through swollen eyes, all my friends watching, taking in the spectacle of me now splattered on the ground. It was their first inkling as to my secret life at home. I wanted to disintegrate into nothingness then. Why was I ever born? Death was better than this. And then I ran away. I ran to a woman's house -- my mother's friend. I told her what had happened and she let me spend the night.

That next morning I got up and went straight to school, where I ran into one of my brothers. He told me that our mother was looking for me. She heard that I was in school and was on her way to get me. I didn't want her to humiliate me again, so I went home to face her. I truly thought she would whip me as soon as I walked through the door, but she didn't. She told me to go to my room.

I was sixteen years old then. I sat in my bedroom, looked out the window and started day-dreaming. It wasn't always like this. Then my thoughts floated through the window, across the years of abuse and molestation and grief …

Far away to a happier, gentler time …

Chapter 2

Beloved

In the mid-1950s my four brothers and I lived with our mother and father in Chicago. Before long they parted ways and my mother took us to Tupelo, Mississippi, to live with our grandparents until our mother got back on her feet, financially speaking. At the time she believed that moving us to Mississippi was in our best interest.

When our mother left our dad I was only three months old, or so I was told. As a single mother, she struggled with raising all of us. Although she had challenges embedded within her, she was still a very good mother and wonderful housewife. We always had good food on the table, clean clothing and we were well taken care of; but ultimately she decided that raising five children on her own was too much for her. I believe that she seemed to be naïve and practically blinded by her own understanding of love. As arrangements were being made to send us to our grandparents, she pursued another man whom she believed was her soulmate and would provide a stable life for all of us.

In Tupelo, my grandparents took us in with open arms and lots of love. They never once made us feel uncomfortable or afraid. On the contrary, we felt protected and secure. Those were good days. We were very young and enjoyed a new life in a new state in a loving, caring home. We were the beloved.

Tupelo, Mississippi, the hometown of Elvis Presley, hosted approximately 17,000 residents was at the time Lee County's governmental center. The weather in Tupelo was different than any other part of the country. The air was hot and humid. Rain soaked the soil in the spring and in the winter it could drop below freezing, and yet it hardly ever snowed.

Whites and Blacks lived in this tiny town and segregation was rampant, even after school segregation became illegal in May of 1954. Furthermore, the Civil

Rights Act of 1957 gave everyone the right to vote but even nowadays one still has to be careful in Tupelo, Mississippi, and all other states for that matter. However, my brothers and I were never aware of this turmoil going on all around us. We had the sweetest grandparents anyone could ever have. We were well cared for and sheltered. As I sit here and ponder my past, I remember those wonderful times.

One day at our grandparents' home, I was playing outside with one of my brothers, whereupon he asked me, alarmed, "What's that on your face?" He took the corner of his shirt, spat on it and tried to wipe my face, shouting, "It won't come off! It just want come off!"

That's when I ran into the house and looked to see what was on my face. In the mirror I saw four, tiny red spots on my face, two on each side. I didn't know what they were so I ran into the kitchen to our grandmother crying, "Grandma' what are these things on my face?"

I remember Grandma' laughing and telling me they were only freckles. "God gave them to you because you're special." After that conversation with Grandma' I went back outside to play with my brother, happy and content. Grandma and Grandpa always had a way of making everything right in the world. My brothers and I played outside most days making mud pies and watching the ants build their homes. We thought them so amazing.

One day, my dad came to visit us unexpectedly in Tupelo. For the next two decades my dad and I talked many times by phone and he always made it seem as though he was right there with me.

I used to love watching my grandma' cook in her kitchen. Sometimes she let me help by stirring the corn-bread and making homemade biscuits, cakes, cookies and pies, just to name a few things. Grandpa' was really our step-grandfather but he was wonderful to us.

He was employed as a cotton-picker, like everyone in those days. I remember always wanting to pick cotton too, so Grandpa' made me a sack out of a pillow-case with a strap on it. Then he took me with him to work in the field. I was so happy picking cotton along-side Grandpa.' Once our bags were filled we hauled them to a place called *the cotton gin*. That's where they paid the pickers according to the weight of the bags. My grandfather told me that I had earned fifty cents that day. I was so happy! Grandpa' asked me what I'd like to buy "with all that money" and I replied, "Peanuts and a soda pop!" and that's sure what he got me. That day was one of the best days of my young, innocent life. It felt great working in the field alongside my beloved grandpa.' I even had enough money left over to attend the county fair.

Grandpa' took us to the county fair where we saw lots of exciting things and people. My favorite television character was there -- *Annie Oakley* -- who played a cowgirl. *Annie Oakley* wore a cowgirl outfit, cowboy boots for girls and two guns strapped to her sides. I watched all her shows on TV with actor, *Gene Autrey*, who played cowboy *Roy Rogers* on his weekly television show. As such, my grandparents bought me a cowgirl outfit to wear to the fair. I was so happy that day, proudly sporting my new outfit!

Our grandparents allowed me and my brothers to run around excitedly all over the fair, looking at everything, eating everything and jumping on all the rides. We were so tired that day that we fell asleep on the horse-and-buggy ride. I was really afraid of horses and mules back then because once my brother tried to mount a horse. He fell under it and the horse almost stomped him. My grandfather grabbed him just in time. After I saw that, I didn't want to ride on horses or mules.

Eventually, I noticed something strange about Tupelo. I couldn't understand why my grandparents always had to say, "Yes sir, and yes ma'am," to the Caucasians in our world. Furthermore, whenever white people walked next to us downtown, we were required to step off the sidewalk, onto the road, and allow them to pass by. I asked my grandfather about these things many times as we walked downtown and to get my mind off the subject, he usually bought me some candy.

He avoided answering such questions because he knew I wouldn't understand prejudice and segregation, nor did he want to introduce me to such ugly things at my tender age. One day, he finally explained, "Well, that's how we have to show respect to the white people." Grandpa' often took us to church with a Bible in one hand and a shotgun in the other.

Chapter 3

Darkness Falls

One day everything changed. I vaguely remember our grandparents sitting all of us down in the living-room to inform us that our mother was coming to Tupelo to take us back and live with her. This time we were going to St. Louis, Missouri, to live with our mother and her new husband. At that time I was four and a half years old and I didn't know my mother. She was like a stranger to me. I only knew my grandparents.

She was now married to a man who was also a stranger to me and my siblings. Apparently, they had been living in Chicago all this time, then moved to St. Louis, where the man bought a home for us to live in. He also owned a variety store directly across the street from the house. And so our mother came to get us.

She called us all into our grandparents' living-room whereupon she introduced herself and her husband as our new parents. She put her arms around us and I felt a momentary sense of comfort.

She also had a beautiful baby girl with her. I looked at the baby and said, "Wow, she looks like a baby doll." I asked my mother who she was, to which she replied, "Why, this is your baby sister!"

I asked if I could hold the baby, so my mother stood behind me in case I dropped her. That's when my baby sister smiled at me, which made me feel really good. Her little smile meant that she loved me and was comfortable around me. I instantly fell in love with this little baby.

At first I thought I was the only one being moved to St. Louis but once I learned that my brothers were going as well, I felt much better. However, my mother took only three of my brothers. My oldest brother stayed behind with my grandparents until he was fifteen. You see, my grandma's health was failing and she needed someone to help her around the house while Grandpa' went to work the cotton fields. With great sadness in our hearts, my brothers and I gave our grandparents a big hug and a goodbye kiss, and told them how much we loved them. Those were the best years of our young lives.

As our new stepfather drove us all to St. Louis, Missouri, I remember riding in the car. It was a long, hot ride, and I kept asking my mother, as all kids do, "Are we there yet?" whereupon she kept us occupied with snacks and toys, as all mothers do.

When we finally arrived at our new house in St. Louis, we saw several kids playing on the street and having fun. Immediately, we wanted to go and play with them but our mother told us to go inside the house first. "Come and see your new rooms and the wonderful new clothes and shoes we bought for you." Well, that got our attention.

Two years went by and my birthday was in January. It was now 1959, whereupon I started school at the age of six, instead of five. I used to cry whenever my mother took me to school. When she left me there, I felt as though she was abandoning me and sneaking off somewhere. I finally got used to it and learned to socialize with the other children. My stepfather had a great job at that time, as well as owning the variety store across the street from our house. My mother was in charge of the store by day and things went very well for our new family during those first few years. And then the darkness fell.

"The devil comes to steal, kill and destroy. But I have come to bring you Life, and that more abundantly."

Christ, John 10:10

Chapter 4

Blinded by Love

Our mother and stepfather started going out occasionally while my older brothers took care of me and my little sister at home. I remember late one night after they came home, hearing our mother and stepfather arguing. I lay in bed in my room listening and eventually fell asleep, but that next morning I saw that our mother's face was badly swollen. I asked her what happened and she said our stepfather had done it. "But he didn't mean it."

Nevertheless, I still didn't understand why he hit her, having never been exposed to such an environment. In fact, whenever they drank, things got out of hand.

One night as I lay sound asleep in my bed, my step-father came into my room and groped my body in the wrong place. I became completely paralyzed with fear. His breath smelled of liquor. His hand was reckless, perverted and aggressive, while my mother was fast asleep in the next room.

I couldn't wait until morning. Surely the warm light of day would bring my mother's rescue. I told her immediately what he had done and to my absolute horror, she dismissed the incident as nothing more than a nightmare. However, in the next breath she actually warned me never to sit in his lap.

I had been violated by my stepfather and deeply betrayed by my mother all in the span of a day. Looking back, she most likely had full knowledge of what her husband was capable of, and yet she never removed me from that house. At the very least she could have taken me back to my grandparents' house.

His visits into my bedroom continued off and on for the next ten years, mostly on weekends. Throughout the next decade I continued to tell my mother about it and she continued to ignore me. I was wounded beyond repair.

Eventually, he disappeared for days on end. Sometimes he came home, sometimes not. Often times I found myself looking in the mirror, wondering how long my mother would endure her relationship with him, as I counted the days for him to leave forever.

School took my mind off things. Upon entering the third grade I was excited to get out of the house, but before long, school became yet another source of torment for me. I was being teased mercilessly by the other kids about the freckles on my face. They called me *the girl with bumps on her face*.

Feeling unattractive at school and worthless at home, I'd go home crying. I tried to smear all kinds of things on my face, hoping the freckles would come off, but nothing ever worked. Although I had looked so forward to going to school, I was now uncomfortable there and even more uncomfortable in my own bedroom.

I never told my brothers about what our stepfather was doing until well later in life. They were older by then and two of them had, in fact, gotten married, while the other two were in and out of the house, engaged in the their own happy, social activities. Besides, had I told them a fight would have ensued against our stepfather and someone would have ended up in jail. And so, always the good daughter, I kept my mouth shut.

My mother, of course, was still in denial. If a parent doesn't believe their own child when soul-crushing events like this occur in the home, to my seven-year old's mind, *no one* would ever believe me. There was no doubt in my mind that it was all my fault. Her denial completely shattered my sense of safety and security. I felt worthless because the one person that was supposed to protect me, continually pushed me away. Her only advice me to me was, *Put your clothes on when you get out of bed and don't sit in his lap*. She knew.

As the years ambled on I began tossing and turning at night. The man continued his visits into my bedroom on weekends and after he left, I just cried and prayed to God to get me out of there. Even as a child I knew his behavior was not right. I was always told that men were not supposed to touch little girls this way, or little boys. Looking back, it seemed that love had blinded my mother against her husband's actions. Did she really think I dreamed all those episodes all those nights? No, I knew it was real and so did she. She was in deliberate denial. She could not accept that someone so dear to her would actually violate her own children. Whenever I tried to get her to help me, she changed the subject and took no steps to do anything about it. No matter how much I cried out, or what I did, I could not get her to help me. And so, I'd go to my bedroom every night and cry.

Then one day, I gained a little hope. My grandmother came to visit us in St. Louis and I thought, if I tell her she might take me back to Tupelo. My grandma' listened but did not respond with the great sense of urgency I expected. She approached my mother but she assured my grandmother that none of it was true. My grandma' left and that was that.

Wasn't there anyone that wanted to help me? In later years as an adult I asked my grandma' why she didn't believe me and she said that my mother had *convinced* her that it wasn't true. So there I was again, a young, hopeless child, trapped in a little girl's body. Sometimes I just sat in my bedroom, looked up toward heaven with tears streaming down my face, asking God, "Why is this happening to me?" I waited for an answer believing that one day he would show up. Although I didn't know too much about God, I did have a little faith in him. I used to pray that God would keep angels around my bedroom. Later in life I learned that he was there all along.

Looking back I can see how he held my life together with his hands and never let go. The evidence of this is because I never turned into a prostitute, never went to jail, never hurt other children and I did, in fact, become a successful business woman.

I needed someone to believe me, someone that I could trust, someone to assure me this would never happen again! Contrary to popular belief, evil can many times overpower the good. We have only to watch the six o'clock news to see how true that is. Take for instance the days of slavery in America, the Jewish Holocaust of the 1940s and children raped and murdered every day in this country. Free will is a devastating thing. It can nurture or kill, tear down or build up.

Shortly after that my stepfather abandoned my mother, at least for a while. By then our mother had brought seven children into this world; two little girls by him. After he left, she was unable to support us and we ended up in our neighbor's garage.

Chapter 5

The Garage

The garage was freezing and the weather was freezing. The year was now 1961 and I was eight years old. It snowed the first week we moved into our dilapidated shack and all we had was one electric heater to keep us warm. My mother slept in a bed with my two sisters while I slept on the freezing, cold floor with my four brothers. The garage was not equipped with a bathroom or kitchen so we had to go into the owner's house to cook and bathe. Sometimes we'd use a hot plate. The entire time that we lived in this garage we fought off cockroaches and rats all around us.

After we lost our home and the store our quality of life took a drastic, downward spiral, but our mother tried to hold us all together and took care of us as well as she could. She also reached out to others in the neighborhood, friends and loved ones for assistance.

While living in the garage, I fell very ill. I couldn't eat and my stomach was swollen like an Ethiopian. I was taken to the hospital whereupon the doctor said I had walking pneumonia. In fact, he said I could have died. The doctor also said my brother and I had asthma, but God intervened and healed our bodies. We lived this way for two years. In any case, our medical condition served as a wake-up call for my mother.

She finally reached out to the community for help. She sent a letter to the Reverend Cleopus Robinson, a well-known pastor in St. Louis. After reading the letter, Reverend Robinson went on the radio and asked the community to drop by the garage and help us. Before the broadcast he invited my mother to come down to the radio station but she declined, whereupon he announced our situation on air, absent of her.

And then here came all the people! Hordes of caring people came knocking at our door! As soon as they walked into our run-down garage they gave us big hugs and loaded us with bag after bag of everything we needed; money, food, warm clothing and supplies! God was changing things around. In fact, these people *over-whelmed* us with their generosity.

After that, we able to move into an apartment almost immediately. My mother packed up everything and with the help of the church members the move very quickly. We were also featured in the newspaper, highlighting where we used to live and how the church members helped rescue us. The church's generosity was inspiring and I will never forget the support they gave us.

Throughout our entire internment in that garage, our mother was unemployed. She also wrote a letter to President Dwight D. Eisenhower. In the letter, she explained our living situation, but no one really knows if he ever read it. Whatever the case, we were able to get help from welfare. My mother never knew that she was entitled to receiving public assistance until then!

And so we moved into a better neighborhood and better housing. The apartment had enough bedrooms for all of us; one for my mother, another for my four brothers complete with bunk-beds, and a third bedroom for me and two sisters. We were overjoyed going into our own rooms and having a real bathroom and kitchen again! At the age of ten, I got on my knees and thanked the Lord.

I've always loved the feel of warm water against my skin. It makes my feet and body feel wonderful, so that weekend I took a long, warm bath; but I wished that that the warm water had washed away all the memories of the past. So I told God, *I believe in my heart there are better days to come.*

Chapter 6

The Burning Bed

After we moved into our new apartment, our stepfather came back around on occasion. One particular night he and my mother went out and didn't come home until late.

That next morning I awakened to the smell of smoke in the house. I walked into the hallway and noticed smoke coming from my mother's bedroom where she lay sound asleep. As I entered her room, I saw smoke soaring upward from her bed, with a smoldering hole in the mattress right next to her head, growing larger by the second! She had fallen asleep with a lit cigarette.

I screamed and tried to wake her up but she just wouldn't wake up. So I ran into my brothers' room and screamed very loudly. "Wake up! Wake up! Mom's bed is on fire and she's gonna' burn to death!"

My brothers jumped out of bed, ran into our mother's room and saw the smoke. They pulled our co-matose mother out of bed whereupon she hit the floor. Then she woke up, yelling, "What's going on?!" My brothers ran into the kitchen to get a bucket of water and they put out the fire within seconds. They were he-roes that day.

We could have all died in that fire but God woke me up so that I could get help for my mother. My brothers dragged the damaged mattress out into the alley and the fire department didn't have to come at all. Thank God for his surrounding angels protecting us.

That morning, our mother finally woke up. I fixed her some coffee but she was still in a daze. You see, what actually happened was, my stepfather had dropped by the apartment the night before and took her out for a couple of drinks, but earlier that evening she had taken medication, which should never have been mixed with alcohol.

One day my mother helped me with my homework. I was now in the sixth grade and on this particular occasion, our assignment was to write a story about how we spent the summer. My mother wrote the entire story for me. Then she told me to rewrite it in my own hand, but I didn't do as she instructed. Instead, I simply added my name to it and gave it to the teacher.

Naturally, my teacher asked me who wrote the assignment and I told her that I did. She said, "No, Dorean, you didn't write this because the writing is too good." She didn't believe me and sent me to the principal's office, whereupon my mother was called to come and get me. She was very angry with me and I thought she'd whip me, but she didn't.

"Dorean, didn't I tell you to rewrite it?"

"Yes, mama."

"Honey, you can't fool the teachers. They know your hand-writing!"

"Yes, mama."

My error in judgment gave me a lesson that I'll never forget. It seemed like our relationship was getting much better at that point. We were living in a much better situation and I could see that our mother tried to keep it that way. She always made sure that we had clean clothes to wear, good food on the table and she used to fix our hair before sending us off to school.

The years went by and I was now fifteen. Our stepfather had started coming around again more frequently and whenever he did, my mother's rage toward me re-emerged, which resulted in her beating me again.

I felt like a punching bag. I couldn't understand why I was getting hit so much, too many times to count, while my brothers and sisters never were! In later years another theory crossed my mind. Perhaps she blamed me for ruining her marriage. Her judgment was so skewed at this point, perhaps she saw me as *the other woman out to steal her man.* It's not the first time that a mother blamed her child for ruining her marriage.

Before long our mother had yet another baby girl, her third child by our stepfather; a total of eight children that she could barely afford. She was in the hospital delivering her eighth baby when our stepfather came to stay at our apartment during her absence. Meantime, I was thinking, *Why is he back here again!*

On one occasion he was taking a shower. He called out through the bathroom door, asking me to hand him a clean towel. I didn't want to and tried to ignore him. Then he called me again. This time I relented and got him the towel. When I knocked on the bathroom door, he opened it, grabbed my arm, and tried to pull me inside. I started screaming but no one heard me because my brothers and sisters were all outside. Then I started crying whereupon he finally let go of my arm. I fell back onto the floor and then ran outside.

That evening I fell into a deep, visible depression because our stepfather was still in the house. I finally told one of my brothers what he had done. My brother, now taller and stronger at the age seventeen confronted him. Shortly after that, the man moved out for good. And that's all it took; just one confrontation, just one person standing up for me.

However, after that confrontation I never told any of my brothers again. Two of them were adults and already married. I knew they'd go after him and I didn't want them to go to jail. Rather, I wanted my mother to put him out of the house, but she loved him without conditions or requirements. Therefore, I was alone again in the nightmare once again.

I used to say to myself, *I wish my stepfather would leave my mom, and never come back.* I used to pray and ask God to give my mother another husband, one who didn't want to harm her children, especially little girls. I wanted my mother to marry a man that loved the Lord, knew how to be a great husband, and one who knew how to be a real father to her children.

My mother finally came home from the hospital with my new baby sister. The doctor told her that, regretfully, my baby sister was mentally retarded and that she would always have the mental capacity of a three-year old. Today, my sister is fifty-two and still living.

During this time, my sisters and I attended church. Our mother finally joined our church while our stepfather once again disappeared from the scene. Predictably, the beatings also stopped, but things started getting really tight again, financially speaking; which meant less food for us kids to eat, less warm clothing, and less money to pay the bills. Many of us kids had jobs by then, including me, so we all chipped in.

The older I got, the more confused I became. I wondered, *What is love?* I never heard my mother tell me that she loved me, that I was pretty or that she was proud of me. I used to wonder why I'm the only one that got all the beatings and cursings. What was going on here was not my fault but I still blamed myself.

Even at that young age, I tried to reason with her many times and point out her mistakes but she refused to hear any of it. I ran away from home a few times but she always found me. I hated coming back home. I just wasn't a happy child there, which is an understatement. I used to walk down the street and never smile. People asked me why I never smiled, so I smiled for them just to shut them up, but in my mind I would say, *If only you knew why I'm not smiling, then you'd understand why there's nothing to smile about.*

Chapter 7

Outcast

Although I still got teased about the freckles on my face, I loved going to school and being around kids my age. It was a place of escape for me. Playing with the kids helped me to block out the things that were going on at home, and took the attention off my hemorrhaging heart. However, over time the sexual and emotional abuse I suffered at home took a toll on me and, more often than not, I found myself unable to cope.

As discussed earlier, my stepfather moved out but he still came around to see my mother. One day she wasn't feeling well, suffering of asthma and high blood pressure. She had just taken her medication again when my stepfather dropped by the apartment and asked her out.

My mother agreed and they left. She didn't return home until the next morning, which happened to be Thanksgiving Day. Again she was passed out in bed the next morning, in no condition to get up and cook a Thanksgiving dinner. So I decided to cook for the entire family. Surely this would bring a smile to her face. Surely this would make her love me and see what a good daughter I was.

That day I cooked the entire Thanksgiving meal, consisting of a delicious turkey, dressing, potato salad, yams, plus mac' and cheese. I even baked a cake and pie! My mother had always taught me how to cook food from scratch and that's one thing I can sincerely give her credit for. She took the time to teach me how to cook all kind of meals. I created a whole Thanksgiving dinner with all the trimmings. I wanted to make sure that my sisters and brothers had a wonderful, memorable Thanksgiving, just like all the other kids. I cooked enough for twelve people or more! The food turned out absolutely delicious and I felt proud of myself for this accomplishment. The looks on my siblings' faces were priceless! I saw contentment in their eyes as they munched and gobbled away, having a wonderful holi day just like all their friends. Yes, my mother would be so proud of me!

Once everyone was finished enjoying Thanksgiving dinner, I didn't want my mother to wake up to a dirty kitchen, so I made sure everything was washed and put away. I even mopped the floors. My mother was still asleep when I went into her room to ask if I could go to the movies with a male friend of mine. As I sat on the edge of the bed waiting for an answer, she lifted the covers back and started screaming at me and calling me names. "No! You *cannot* go out with that boy!" The look on her face was that of one who didn't know where she was or who she was talking to!

Then she accosted me. She cursed and beat me, this time so badly, that my face swelled up. In fact, my face was so badly hurt, I could not go to school for the next two weeks. I looked like a monster. My mother called the school and told them I was sick. If only they knew what was really going on in our house.

I couldn't understand what brought on this rage! I simply asked a question. *Can I go out to the movies with my friend?* I made sure the house was clean and my brothers and sisters were fed. The least she could have done was let me go out as a reward. With a great deal of with shame, I called and told my friend that I couldn't go out with him. I didn't want anyone to see me with my face like that.

My mother fell asleep again and when she woke up later that evening, I brought a plate of dinner into her bedroom, whereupon she gasped in horror when she saw my face. "Oh my God! Who did that to you!?"

I was dumbfounded. She didn't remember that she had done it. Immediately she grabbed me, which scared me, because I thought I was going to get hit again, but she didn't. I answered very softly, "You did this to me, Mommy, when I asked you if I could go out with my friend!"

My mother held onto me tightly and told me how very sorry she was for doing that to my face. Growing up as a child I tried to draw closer to her but the more distant she became. Instead she got closer to my brothers and sisters. I was the outcast.

The feeling of being rejected by someone you love is unbearable, especially if the one that should have loved me the most, didn't -- or didn't know how to show it. I thought, since she was the one that brought me into this world, I could expect her to love me. At that moment when she held me and expressed how sorry she was, I looked at her with a blank stare on my face. It was as if my mother wanted me to tell her that someone else had done this to me. Once she came to grips with what she had done, she broke down crying, and said over and over, "I'm so sorry, I'm so sorry!" She promised never to drink again. And to her credit, she was actually telling the truth. She never drank again.

I now understand that not everyone knows how to show love and affection. Some people have been hurt and damaged themselves, and do the best that they can. I thank God that I didn't inherit this hatred and negative influence. I believe that my mother loved me in her own special way. I just didn't understand her method, because love is supposed to be something good and wonderful, but I never felt it coming enough from her, although I wanted to so badly. I knew deep down in her heart, she was trying to raise all of us the best she could.

I knew she had suffered a lot of disappointments in her own life; even as a child I could see and feel her suffering. She had to deal with eight children; three by my stepfather and five by my biological father, practically all alone. Our real father was an artist who consistently stayed on the road because of his singing gigs. Therefore, out of her pain, she reached out to another man, my stepfather, whom she believed would help her emotionally, financially, and help to raise her children. However, that sequel ended in total devastation and put us all into a roach-infested garage.

Many women look for love in the wrong places to fill that void within them, but they soon realize that when they reach out from hurt, they can potentially get even more hurt. They fall in love with certain men, hoping to receive the proper love and guidance in return, but those individuals don't always show them how to cope with life; nor do those dream-boat men point to things that make them whole. For instance, my mother's mother and father were not together, and my mother was also raised without her mother.

I could tell that there was something within my mother that wanted to do right, because she loved going to church. She went to church with us regularly, but for some reason, whenever she got home her personality took a drastic turn. Don't get me wrong, I loved my mother unconditionally and I can truly say that in later years we did have some good days. Sometimes my mother and I would laugh and enjoy ourselves and other times she would just snap. As I got older, I realized that my mother's abuse toward me as a child was actually a spiritual battle. If people don't get the proper guidance to get them back on the right track, they will never realize that they have a sickness that can devastate the lives of others. Nowadays they call this disease bi-polar disorder. Bipolar disorder, also known as manic-depressive illness, is a brain disorder; the symptoms of which can be severe. She was in need of medical attention and never received it, because back then treatments were not as common as they are today. Back then I didn't know what was going on. I blamed myself.

Chapter 8

The Phone Call

I continued to pray every day, went to school and took care of my little sisters whenever I could. My older siblings were now in their early twenties and took care of themselves. I didn't have any money to go to all the popular places. like concerts with my friends, but I did get the opportunity to go to the movies Back then the trend was going to drive-through movies and then over to someone's house-party. I was able to do that maybe twice a year. The rest of my time was spent taking care of my younger siblings and the house.

Around 1970, I got my first job at Woolworth's as a cashier and customer service representative. I was the only Black, teenage girl working there at the time.

I really enjoyed this job, especially when the manager informed us that we could accept tips from customers; so we kept a jar at the counter. Some of the customers were really nice and gave us tips. At the end of the week the manager took the tips and split them among us. As the months went by we encountered a young, female co-worker who was stealing money out of the tip jar and by the end of each week the jar was almost empty.

This same girl lied and told the manager that *I was the one* stealing the money and that she saw me take it. The manager confronted me about this and I thought, *This cannot be happening to me!* Just when things were looking brighter for me, now this! I tried to explain to the manager and my co-workers that what she was saying wasn't true, but they didn't believe me. They believed her and fired me.

I was very hurt and felt like I was let down yet again, with what little hope I had left. So I prayed about this. A month went by and they finally found out that it really wasn't me stealing tips from the jar. They realized it was her all along and that my statement was true! Therefore, they decided to hire me back but my feelings were still very badly hurt. I told my mother that I didn't want to go back there ever again and face them. They made me feel ashamed and then tried to rehire me as though nothing happened. I wasn't having any of that. They too had betrayed my trust, so I never went back. But I didn't give up hope; I just gave up on them.

I ending up landing another job working at the local Health Care Center. It was seasonal and I worked there only for the summer. All the money I made went toward paying the bills and groceries for the family. I rarely hung out with other teenagers and kept making excuses when they'd ask me out. The truth was, I didn't have any money to go out with them. I could never buy myself anything new and always shopped at the local thrift stores to buy clothes, until well after I moved out my mother's house.

High school graduation was soon approaching, which I dreaded, because it was evident that I couldn't afford my graduation robe, ring and photos, not to mention going to the prom. By then I landed a decent job, for a teenager, working at the federal building as a file clerk. I should have been happy to get paid but every payday my mother came to my place of work to pick up my money. She needed it to help pay the rent. I was just working to pay bills, but in a way I didn't really care. I loved my job because it was an escape for me to get away from home.

Having no money wasn't really all that bad. I was just happy to give my siblings a better life. The thought of life back in that infested garage to me was terrifying. Although many times I wished that I could have saved money to buy myself something nice, or go to places with other teens my age, I was not able to because I just worked so hard all the time.

I now had to think about my future. I began seeking God for a way of escape, so I prayed that I could receive a scholarship because my biological parents didn't have the money to send me to college. So I took the first step of faith and set up an appointment with my high school counselor. She asked me a series of questions, one of which was -- what did I want to major in?

For a moment, it seemed like boldness took over me, so I looked her in the eyes and said with great confidence, "I want to be a news reporter." She replied, "OK, you need to find a college that offers journalism."

My biological father, aunt, uncle and cousins lived in

Chicago so I began looking for colleges there. I felt like I was actually doing something productive to improve my life! I loved my father because whenever we talked on the phone I felt a sense of security. He seemed to harbor a genuine love for me.

Then an idea hit me. I should call my aunt in Chicago but I didn't want her phone number showing up on our phone bill; otherwise my mother would have gotten suspicious and flipped out. Suddenly the idea to call my aunt *collect* shot through my mind. This way my aunt's phone number could not be traced back to my mother's phone bill.

Months went by and I finally worked up the courage to sneak that collect call. My mother stepped out of the house one day and that's what prompted me to do it. I prayed very hard that she would not walk in and catch me talking about her on the phone, especially to my father's side of the family. But I just had to tell someone, anyone that would listen! Hoping my aunt would accept my call, I quickly dialed her number and … she answered! And then I told her *everything!*

I told her about my mother's husband molesting me for the past decade. I told her that I believed my mother seemed to know about the molestation and did nothing about it, and I told her about my mother hitting, punching and knocking me to the ground at home and in front of my friends. Then I asked if I could write her a letter describing everything that happened at my mother's house since the time we moved to St. Louis. I finally had enough and used every ounce of strength within me to tell someone.

My aunt, of course, got very angry. Here was an adult that finally wanted to stand up for me, but I pleaded with her not to mention any of this to my mother. God had to be with my aunt during the next few months because she didn't breathe a word of it to my mother.

I asked her to watch for the letter coming from me and also asked her to tell my father that I wanted to come and stay with him and go to college in Chicago. She promised that she would do all I asked and I felt a deep sense of security knowing she would convey my messages. Then I told her that if she didn't tell my father to send for me, I would kill myself.

My aunt agreed and I quickly hung up my mother's phone. I finally had someone who listened, someone I could trust. I felt a little hope during that time, but the specter of abuse still coursed through my mind.

Shortly after that I was granted a scholarship from Central YMCA Community College in Chicago to attend their School of Journalism. When the scholarship award letter arrived I was ecstatic. I ran to tell my mother the good news and showed her the letter. I was waiting for her to rejoice and tell me how proud she was of me. Instead, her response was, "Dorean, why would you want to take up journalism? No one is going to hire you in that profession." I told her that I wanted to be a news reporter. She replied, "You should take something else because no one's gonna' consider hiring a Black person to interview them."

Although, talking to my aunt and receiving this scholarship was exhilarating, my mother just sucked it right back out of me. I felt so bad. All I wanted was for her to give me a great, big hug and tell me how proud she was of me. She could have supported me in becoming the first African-American news reporter but as always, she let me down again. There was just no end to her disappointing me. I went into my room and prayed to God about ways to make my mother believe in me, and how to please her until she could love and support me. Nothing that I did pleased her. *Maybe when I leave she'll be happy.*

That night I stayed in my room until it was time for dinner. After dinner, I went straight to bed; my emotions had gotten the best of me. It seemed as though I was the only one that was happy and excited for me. I ached for my father to call my mother. I just wanted to leave, but he took way too long to answer.

Chapter 9

Graduation Massacre

In 1973 I turned eighteen. At the graduation ceremony I remember looking around the facility and didn't see any of my family members. No one came to my graduation; not my mother, brothers or sisters. I was terribly hurt and ashamed. All my friends and teachers asked me, "Dorean, are your parents here? Did any of your family come?"

I looked around and saw the families of all my classmates surrounding them and supporting them with congratulations, hugs and photographs to commemorate that precious occasion that might never come again. By contrast my own family life was horrific, humiliating. I just couldn't understand why my mother didn't come to see me graduate! She made sure to show up on payday to confiscate my payroll but couldn't bring herself to see me graduate from high school! I called home to find out if she was maybe running late. That's when my sister told me she took off with my stepfather to buy a new car. That day the effects of all the neglect washed over me like a tidal wave.

I had finally come to what should have been a joyous stage of my life but the pain and anguish just wouldn't let me go, not even here, not even on my graduation day. I just wanted all of this to be over, I wanted out, I wanted away!

It seems like everyone I was associated with was oblivious to the fact that their behavior was crushing me. I was shaped and molded, not by love and nurture, but by repeated abuse and abandonment that robbed me of my childhood and every shred of self-esteem.

Nevertheless, I began to say to myself, "I need to keep moving forward in life! I have to encourage myself even when others don't believe in me. I just can't give up now! I have to move forward! I can't stay here crippled by the circumstances of life! I have to pursue my own happiness and become successful!"

God gave me multiple talents and all I needed was encouragement and a good plan. Oftentimes, I found myself like David in the Bible, conquering my giants and had to encourage myself. That gave me the strength to move forward.

Growing up, my heart was into creative writing. Back then Negroes were not allowed to hold certain jobs or be in certain places because of segregation during the first half of the 20th century. Dr. Martin Luther King. Jr. had brought about many significant changes by raising the American social conscience about peace, inequality and injustice; even long after his assassination in April of 1968. As a result, there were many things to write about and this is what inspired me to become a reporter. It's also why media became my passion. More specifically, I always dreamed of being a writer who would interview celebrities.

So there I was at my graduation and no one showed up. I was all alone. I remember being so hurt that I walked down the street, diploma in my hand, with tears streaming down my face. What could I do to win someone's love when it seemed like I didn't even exist? The truth was, my mother loved my stepfather more than me and she proved it over and over. I thought that the emotional damage was over at last, but to my despair it started all over again.

Walking down the street that day I suffered yet another bout of chronic depression whereupon my self-worth crashed to the bottom. In today's vernacular it's called clinical depression.

And by the way, why has my father not yet contacted me yet?

The trauma of those years rushed over me then, like the ebb and motion of some dark, muddy sea. I proceeded down the street toward the bus stop, tears still running down my face, and just as I was about to step on the bus, my sister-in-law drove up in her car and called out my name. Happy and relieved, I jumped into her car, whereupon she informed me that she had left a message with my mother that I was going to spend the night at her house. My brother, sister-in-law and their little family, actually took the time to prepare a graduation dinner for me on my special day. I was so very grateful. The terrible events of the day were intercepted by someone in my family that actually cared about me, and all it took was one simple dinner and a hug!

When I got home, my mother demanded that I clean up the house, wash clothes and cook dinner. Graduation day was already ruined so what difference did it make? I did my chores right up to bedtime. She never once mentioned my graduation. It was time for me to leave. The last straw had finally come.

Dear God, when will my dad finally call? What's taking him so long? Too much time went by waiting for his call and I began to feel trapped all over again. I wondered if any of my friends went through similar things that I endured. My mind was challenged by this question day by day. If they had, they never shared that information with me, or maybe, like me, they were also too ashamed to talk about it.

Then one day the phone rang.

I was cleaning house and had almost forgotten the letter I sent my dad and aunt. I'd had enough of waiting. Then the phone rang a second time and I picked it up. It was my father.

He called to ask my mother if I could come and live with him in Chicago. Immediately, my mother told him no. Furthermore, she actually had the audacity to demand that my biological father get *permission* from my stepfather!

My dad became outraged by this demand and screamed at her through the phone. Apparently he must have threatened her somehow because, suddenly obedient, she handed me the phone. He asked if I wanted to come and live with him in Chicago and I said, "Yes!" Then he told me to put my mother back on the phone. At that moment a joy, an empowerment, came over me that I hadn't experienced since my happier days with my grandparents. In fact, I had forgotten what happiness was. Oh, how I praised God that day!

My dad came through for me and arrangements were made for him to send me a bus ticket. However, I never received that money. My mother made sure of that.

Chapter 10

Trapped

I was turning nineteen, I was fed up and ready to go. I was a young woman ready to take control of my own life and I was excited at my prospects ahead.

After my dad called, I cried from the depth of my being, praising God for the miracle of his call and delivering me out my situation. Endless relief gushed from my soul day after day, like the cool waters of a crystal stream. To my mind I would no longer be trapped ever again. Still, the illusion of happiness, like the fleeting wind, many times came and went. Nevertheless I couldn't wait to leave. I was on my way to Chicago!

I started packing my clothes early, days ahead of time. Right around that time, my sister-in-law came over and we decided to walk over to her house for a while. As we started walking over there, my mother decided to come along, uninvited.

At my brother's home, I talked about the trip to Chicago endlessly and excitedly. Then I happened to mention that my dad was going to send me the money to help me get there. That's when my mother's rage erupted once again. She jumped up from her seat, and with a new kind of anger in her voice, she spat, "I can fix it so you can't go! If he sends you that money, I can fix it so you can't go nowhere!"

This was below the belt, even for her. We were all shocked, speechless. When she made this threat I actually believed it. Immediately, I went into overdrive and plotted my escape. *What am I going to do?! What if I can't go to Chicago?! I will lose my scholarship!*

I went home that night, got on my knees and asked God to help me escape from my mother's house. I felt trapped again. What if she makes good on her promise and tries to make me stay? That night I managed to fall asleep, somehow. That next morning, my mother's threat still rang in my head. *I can fix it so you can't go! If he sends you money, I can fix it so you can't go nowhere!*

So I got up and secretly called my brother. I asked him to buy me a one-way, Greyhound ticket to Chicago. I also told him to tell our mother that Dad would mail the ticket to his house. This way she couldn't take the money and spend it on herself. My brother agreed and bought the ticket. I woke up the next morning and got ready to leave, with a new kind of resolve, a new kind of indignation.

The day I left, my mother was silent to me. I wanted her to go with me to the Greyhound station and tell me how much she would miss me and hated to see me go, like other parents. Instead, she curled up on the couch with her back turned away from me. I went over to her and kissed her on the cheek but she never turned around. It really disturbed her that I was leaving. I felt a new mixture of emotions that day; sadness, knowing that I'd have to leave my beloved, little sisters behind, and yet great peace, because I had survived. How much grief can one heart take? I was finally free, no longer trapped. I walked out the door with my bags and never looked back.

Chapter 11

Child of Destiny

As the Greyhound rolled away that spring day with a low hum, it rocked back and forth in a soothing motion, cradling everyone onboard. I was finally happy but still terribly confused. Why was I made a target for pain and anguish? What was it about me that my mother loathed so deeply?

It would soon be revealed, unbeknownst to everyone and even me, that I was a child of destiny. From the moment I was born, God had preordained my destiny. The devil smelled it all over me and tried to kill it. He tried to kill Jesus too, during the Bethlehem Massacre of Matthew Chapter 2. So I guess I'm in good company. Funny thing about destiny; it fulfills itself whether your enemies like it or not.

The bus headed out of St. Louis toward the open highway of the American Midwest. Then my thoughts drifted over the landscape of my life, back into the eclectic kitchen of the home I left behind.

How well I used to clean the house and take care of my little sisters. I contributed to the household with money and groceries and cooked meals for the family whenever I could. We had a credit account at the store that we paid every month. I pushed a shopping cart, sometimes two, full of groceries back to our house and sometimes my little sister came along.

As discussed earlier, my younger sister was, and still is, mentally retarded. She got sick a lot and often had seizures, whereupon we had to stick a spoon in her mouth to prevent her from swallowing her tongue. Her body jerked as though struck by lightning and, of course, many times I was the one that had to deal with the stress of her infirmities. I loved her so much but I was only a teenager, but by the grace of God I made it through all that, but it pushed me into adulthood far too early in life.

Still on the bus, I thought back to the time when I gave my pastor's wife a glimpse of what was going on at our house, whereupon she and the pastor lifted me up in prayer. Then they sought out my mother and spoke to her about the abuse, after which she thrashed the living daylights out of me when we got home.

"Don't you *ever* talk to *anyone* ever again about what goes on in *my* house!" she screamed.

She became unhinged several times about this, as she suspected that I was telling them things. She was correct. I had to tell someone because it was killing inside. Many times I tried to seek out ways to kill myself because I couldn't take it anymore.

One day I went into my mother's bedroom and saw her bottle of medication. I looked at it, planned to take the whole thing, and die. So I went to my closet, kneeled and prayed. I cried and prayed and cried and prayed, meaning to take the pills and end it all.

Suddenly, I heard a loud knock at the front door. My friend came to tell me about a revival that was going on at the church where I attended. Immediately, I wiped my eyes and ran to ask my mother if I could go. To my surprise she said yes!

At the revival, an evangelist preached. He walked up to me, touched my head and prayed for me. He told me that I would be a great leader one day for young people. He also said that he saw some 'fame' in my life.

I never forgot the message he gave me that day. As I received the words he spoke, he began to pray over me more earnestly and that's when the Holy Spirit fell on me and I fell to the floor praising God!

After the revival, I nervously walked home. It was late and I didn't want to be in trouble with my mother. Thank God she was sound asleep and didn't wake up. Back in my room, I got on my knees again, thanked God and went to bed. Just as I dozed off my mother barged into my room, smacked on the light and started screaming at the top of her lungs. But who was she screaming at? Was it me? What had I done? I sat straight up in my bed and quivered, "What's going on?"

And that's when I saw him! There he was – my stepfather -- crawling on his hands and knees next to my bed. She had finally caught him!

My mother went berserk! "I finally caught you!" She cursed him out and forced him out of my room. In fact, she made him leave the house that night. Finally it was being revealed that I spoke the truth all along. I felt a great sense of relief and vindication knowing the truth was being exposed. I went to sleep soundly that night, perhaps for the first time in a decade.

It turned out that the anointing was still all over me from the church service earlier that night and the evil in my stepfather could no longer stand up against the Lord in me. There's a lesson here. When we go into the house of God, bondages are broken and evil is revealed.

That next morning, he came back into our house and fear gripped me once again, but he didn't end up staying. He came only to pick up some things he'd left behind. After that, he finally left me alone for good, but by then it was too late. I was already damaged mentally, phyoically and omotionally.

I felt safe in the presence of the Lord, so I stayed in church, worshiped in the choir and worked on concerts and youth activities, which is something that I was good at -- still am. Another of my passions is music.

Just then, the sun set down for the evening over the rolling hills along the highway. Everyone on the bus going to Chicago fell into a twilight hush. Some took out sandwiches and sodas, while others fell asleep, or spoke in quiet whispers. Evening had fallen and in just a few hours, I'd arrive in Chicago.

Chapter 12

Angel at My Side

I loved my mother and brothers and sisters, and I knew they all loved me. I hated to leave them. The Greyhound continued to hum along the open highway through the towns and hamlets of America's Midwest. That's when I began to ponder how my life would have turned out had my stepfather never set foot into my bedroom when I was just seven years old, or if someone had protected me from him. What would my mother's life have been like, had she married a man who knew how to be a father, instead of someone who was out for his own pleasures? Maybe he had problems in his childhood and it just repeated itself onto others?

When I was a child we were not allowed to speak out about things like this, such as someone touching you in the wrong place. How is a child to cope if they can't report the person that is abusing them? And when the child did speak out in those days, nobody believed them until the adults saw it for themselves. Later in life, some turn to drugs, some to illicit sex, others lose their minds because they're not strong enough to bare it.

I thank God that I was one of the few who were able to release it and not keep it inside. Even if no one listened, I was fortunate not to become an abuser. I thank God that he allowed my mother to see it with her own eyes. Maybe she didn't know, after all, judging by her reaction when she finally caught him. Then again, what about her telling me, "Keep your clothes on when you go to the bathroom at night?" Maybe guilt stopped her from saying anything to me the day I left?

Aren't the children's words worth any credit? Do their words fall on deaf ears? Has society become so blinded that if they don't see it, they won't believe it? Young people have a voice too. All too often, mothers fail to stand up to their boyfriends and husbands and end up favoring men over their own children. They end up actually disliking their own children instead of the men who committed the crime!

This is especially true when a daughter tells her mother that the man she loves sexually abused her. It's harder for mothers to accept this when their own man is involved, because now it becomes a jealousy issue. They would rather blame their own flesh and blood than face the truth, until the truth smacks them square in the face. Until then, many mothers will cover it up but the truth eventually comes out.

One day the principal summoned me to come to the office and when I arrived she asked me why I was late so much? She said that I had been late seventy-seven days that year and I really didn't know what to tell her. After offering no explanation she suspended me. Then she said I couldn't come back to school until my mother brought me back. I was devastated. Now I had to tell my mother about my suspension! I prayed to God, asking him to prevent my mother from beating me and, surprisingly, she didn't. Somehow, the Lord touched her heart. But then she asked me and odd question, "Dorean, do you really want to go back to school?" I told her, yes, I did.

On the night of my junior prom, I watched from the window as all my friends paraded down the street, wearing their sparkling, flowing gowns and tuxedos, headed for the prom. Eventually, my mother asked if I was ready to go back to school and I told her I was, so she enrolled me into a better high school.

Because I missed two months of my education due to the suspension, I had to attend high school *and* night school in order to graduate on time, which I completed. Because of the double-schedule, I stayed at my brother's home in order to catch up. This suited me well because I had peace of mind there. It was quiet, I was able to study and that's how I graduated. I went home only on weekends to my mother's house.

The memories continued to flood through my mind as the Greyhound rolled along. The further we traveled away from St. Louis the more excited I became. I was on my way to Chicago where my father, uncles, aunties and cousins were, and I started praising God. Then tears flowed down my face and there was no way to hide them.

Just then, a lady came and sat next to me on the bus and she asked, "Sweetheart, why are you crying?"

I told her a little bit about my story and that I loved my family and my mother unconditionally. The lady then instructed me to pray and ask God to teach me how to forgive everyone that hurt me, and to make sure that I joined a good church when I got to Chicago. I didn't understand why I had to forgive *them* when they are the ones that hurt me, but the lady knew what she was talking about.

She knew that forgiving them was not for their benefit, it was *for mine!* Releasing pain and anger allows us to move forward, live healthy lives and become successful. Forgiveness sets us free. Holding it in causes us to implode. The lady's advice was for me ... *not them!*

I promised the lady that I would do all she advised and then I fell asleep. When I woke up she was gone. The lady was nowhere to be found on the bus! She was an angel at my side.

I looked out the window toward heaven and thought, *I will hold onto the words that the angel of God spoke to me.* And from that point forward everything changed. I had great things to look forward to and I never allowed anyone to disrespect me *ever again.* She was an angel by my side.

Chapter 13

Provision & Protection

To this day I thank God for touching my brother's heart to pay for my Greyhound bus ticket. He used some of the money that he had set aside for his own family in order to buy me the ticket and to this day, he doesn't fully understand that he actually saved my life. Because of his obedience, I am no longer trapped in that little girl's body. I was soon able to release the past, start on my own journey and become purpose-driven.

I remain thankful that God took what the devil meant for evil, and turned it around for my good. We all have a purpose in life that guides us to our destiny. I can say with confidence that my past experience enabled me to build on the hurt, abuse, and neglect and today I stand on a solid foundation. Hence, my purpose-driven dream is to be in a position to help others overcome. The path I was forced to take was not easy, but I was determined not to let it destroy me. God placed a greater love in me that allowed me to overcome the trials I had endured.

As I look over my life, I know there wasn't anyone but God on my side. I would oftentimes have an out of body experience and find comfort hiding in the little girl that didn't want to come out. She just wanted to remain there forever. But God, with a greater purpose, empowered me with strength to overcome.

My plea goes out to all mothers. Please listen to your children. They have voices too. Many times people choose the violator over the victim. Today, I stand before you and ask that you put your child first. I just happened to be fortunate that God stepped in, turned my life around and allowed me to build on my past to have a stronger future. I could have been one of those who turned to many things in an attempt to cover up the hurt.

When a parent and protector betrays us this way, the soul can become shattered, incapacitated. Deep down inside I knew of a Higher Power. The knowledge of Christ was already in my life even at an early age. My grandfather taught us how to pray and how to love people.

Children are born innocent but many times fall into the hands of a darker soul who feels the need to exploit their sick intentions on helpless, vulnerable ones; children more often than not. These darker souls are out for their own gain and don't care that their actions injure others.

We need mothers in the churches to be accessible to children who don't have that mentorship or love in their homes. If you can embrace others that are going through horrific or similar situations, I know that God can and will give you the ability to show forth his love.

I'm thankful for all the people God sent across my path to deposit encouragement in me, with words like ... *Don't give up!* ... *Press your way towards the prize!* ... I'm glad I listened. I've been to many places trying to find my identity in life, but this thing is for sure: I am not my past. I do not blame myself. God comforts me and it's all for my good.

I thank God for my many friends who encouraged me to take that extra step in faith even when I didn't believe in myself. I thank God for the pastor that believed in me and was obedient in delivering the words that God gave him, words that fed my spirit with hope, determination and the tenacity to fulfill my dreams. I thank God for turning my pain into purpose. I thank God for the ability to love my mother and those that hurt me in the past. I thank him for allowing me to have forgiveness in my heart and to have a passion and love for others.

Children don't ask to come into this world. It's God's purpose that the seed is developed and entrusted into the hands of someone who will care for them, nurture, guide and raise them into maturity, so that when trials come their way they are able to overcome. In today's society, it's not only girls being assaulted and abused, but boys too. Parents, listen to your children, pay attention to their behavioral changes. Be sensitive to the silent cry that lurks within and are never expressed on the outside.

I was tired of being sick and tired, and I took that pain, turned it into passion and sought out ways to better myself. I refused to remain a victim when I was called to be a victor! I used my energy to seek out higher education. I watched the company I kept because I didn't want to be around negative people. I was now driven to seek out only positivity, because positive people will always find ways to motivate you to the next level.

In Chicago I had found the school that would set me up for my success and purpose. I would soon be detached from my past and fully linked to my future. I was ready to pursue my education and planned on looking only for those people who were purpose-driven.

God certainly stepped into my life along with his angels to guard, guide and protect me throughout my life. He reminds me daily that he has work for me to do and to not let my past dictate my future. I know it's hard for men and women to open up and speak about molestation in their lives but the fact is, it still exists in so many households today. We need to encourage our children to speak up and speak out.

Sometimes it helps if we place a face to what a person has gone through, cry out, realize they need help, and begin the healing process. Sometimes God covers a person and reveals to others the strength he has given them for an appointed time. I was one of those people who didn't look like what they'd been through. At the end of the day, my purpose is to help you overcome whatever it is you're facing today, and to let you know there is healing after the pain.

Chapter 14

Bullet Through the Wall

It was now the spring of 1974. I was nineteen years old when I arrived at Chicago's Central YMCA Community College for my first day of school. It was thrilling and exhilarating to be there. I was so happy that I practically didn't know what to do!

I stayed at my aunt and uncle's home (my dad's brother). My dad came over to see me and I felt like a little girl all over again. He was the medicine to my pain and I was on my way to healing. I felt safe. My father asked me if I wanted to stay with him and I told him that I wanted to stay with my uncle and aunt because they had children of their own. We used to visit Chicago during the summer vacation and the fact that their kids were my age made it more exciting. Furthermore, my dad rented a room from someone he knew, which was his typical lifestyle because he was on the road a lot singing, and he didn't want a permanent home. Although my dad was very nice I didn't really care to stay with him because in many ways he was still like a stranger. After what I'd been through I needed to build trust.

Immediately, my self-esteem was raised being around these caring people. I now had the confidence to start my college education and take that step of faith toward my career. It helped me to pull myself up mentally.

During my years in college, I became the chief editor of the college newspaper. I was so proud of myself! How much I had accomplished in such little time! I shouted from the top of my lungs and thanked God for healing me beyond my pain. I wanted to prove a point, not just to myself but to my mother as well, so I mailed her several copies of my college newspaper. I was naturally excited and waited with anticipation for her reply but it never came. So I called to see if she had received the editions of my college newspaper. Holding the phone I waited with eager anticipation for her to congratulate me, but her remarks were disappointing.

"Why did you take up something that no one's going to hire you for, because of the color of your skin?"

She didn't express that the articles were interesting or well-crafted. She didn't say, "I'm really proud of you." Instead, she said, "You'll never make it as a news reporter." I just sat there in silence. After I hung up the phone, all I could say was, "Wow, mom!"

She had killed my spirit all over again. I began to relive the past in my mind and suffered flashbacks of myself as a little girl. I thought that I had gotten over these feelings of helplessness but every time I spoke to her I reverted back in time. But I was determined to overcome! I had a dream! I had a goal and nothing and no one could stop me from attempting to achieve it!

I studied two years of journalism. Later I changed my course to business administration. I also got a job at a well-known restaurant, where celebrities came in to eat and hang out. Although it was part-time it was a step in the right direction. My aunt and uncle didn't ask me to go to work but I didn't want to be a burden on them. Besides, I was used to working from a very young age until I became independent. I lived with my aunt and uncle for six months, then moved in with my cousin, the son of my aunt and uncle, for another six months. He and his wife were looking for a babysitter, plus they lived closer to my job. I worked from 12:00 midnight until 7:00 the next morning. I had just enough time to get the kids ready for school. I was very concentrated on my own education and didn't want anything to hinder that; therefore, I understood the importance of theirs.

After I got them off to school, I finished up my studying, then cleaned the house, whereupon my classes ran from 4:00 to 10:00 PM. Immediately after class I went to my job, while my cousin picked up the kids from school in the afternoons. Babysitting the kids was my way of paying rent and it worked out well. I was required to pay only the telephone bill whenever I called long distance. Finally, I had money for myself to do the things I really liked.

I loved going to Gospel concerts with my dad, watching him sing as well as the other great artists, like *The Soul Stirrers, Shirley Caesar, Mighty Clouds of Joy, Mississippi Mass Choir* and, of course, the group my father sang with, *The 5 Tones of Harmony*. He also sang in concert with *The Soul Stirrers.*

My father sang with many Gospel artists, traveled to many places and saw a lot of things that he described whenever we were together. My father's brother (the uncle I stayed with for six months) also sang with *The Original Spiritual Stars.*

I met a young man in my uncle's group who was a musician and he played base. I loved traveling with my uncle to Gospel events. Eventually the young man and I started dating. He was thirty-two, I was twenty-two and I ended up moving in with him. I thought the world of him but what I didn't know was that he loved to drink.

I didn't like that part about him because I had just come out of an abusive household. He was a great provider but when the weekend came he got his cases of beer, rum and coke. He drank on Fridays after work and on Saturday he'd go to group rehearsal.

One day my sister came to Chicago from St. Louis to visit me. We were elated to see each other! My boyfriend and I took her out to dinner and she went to church with me. One night after we all went to bed, I jumped out of bed suddenly and noticed that my boy-friend was not in the bed with me. I went into the living room to see if he was there but he wasn't. So I went to our guestroom where my sister was sleep, and there he was ... standing over my little sister ... naked.

I screamed at him, ran into our bedroom room and pulled his 22-caliber firearm out of the dresser drawer. Then I shot a bullet into the wall over his head. He ran into the bathroom, slammed the door shut and began to plead for his life -- and rightfully so. He didn't know who he as dealing with here. "Please don't shoot me!" he cried over and over. In that moment my past re-emerged and I was once again trapped in that little girl's body, only this time ... she had a gun.

My sister woke up frantic, holding onto the sheets. I thank God that I didn't shoot him that night. I would have ended up in jail and lost my scholarship. From be-hind the bathroom door he continued to plead for his life.

"I'm sorry, I'm so sorry!" Then I told him to leave and he did. That next morning things simmered down and I allowed him back into the apartment. I asked him to drive us over to my aunt's house, so that my sister had a safe place to stay for the rest of the week. After we got home, I had a discussion with my, shall we say, former boyfriend. I told him my story of being molested as a child, how much damage it caused me, and that I would not allow this to happen to any of my siblings. I told him his actions were unacceptable and that his intentions ruined everything between us.

"What would have happened had I not stepped in? This cycle is not going to repeat itself, not if I can help it."

I told him that I no longer felt comfortable with him in my life. The trust I had in our relationship was gone. And I summed it up with, "You're basically lucky to be alive right now."

That night something triggered in me. The prospect of something this devastating happening to someone I love would never be tolerated. "You're also lucky that I didn't call the police and have you arrested."

If I ever saw this happening to anyone, I would never be silent. I would call the police in a heartbeat. "I don't love you anymore and it's time for you to leave."

He pleaded for me to take him back but there was no way. Later my uncle found out what had happened and asked if I wanted to move back into their home. I politely declined because I so desired to be independent and on my own, but he offered that his door would always remain open.

After that I lived by myself for the first time so I got down on my knees and prayed. I had to find a better-paying job to pay bills, now that I was paying rent on my own. I had saved up some money from my college fund and that was enough to carry me through for about a year. My rent was $127 a month, which included lights and gas. I could afford that until another job came along.

I was still trapped in that little girl's body. Every time the woman in me tried to come out, hurt would smack her back inside, therefore, I was always at church, never missed a Sunday and stayed there until my wounds were healed. After that, I didn't have the confidence to date anyone for quite a while. I wanted to make sure that the next man in my life would be sent from God; a God-fearing man who would make me his wife.

Chapter 15

Healing After the Pain

I had always wanted to pursue singing and be in a group. I wanted to be like my uncle and father because they really knew how to stir up a crowd. Just the excitement of being on stage doing something you love was so amazing to me. I was at an event with my uncle's group when a young lady walked up to me and said, "Your uncle's group sounds really great, and so does your dad's." Then she asked, "Do you sing?"

I told her I do, a little, whereupon she introduced herself and said, "I'm with *The Gospelettes* and we're looking for a background singer. Are you interested?"

The Gospelettes were very well-known at the time and still are. I thought, *Is this really happening to me?* My dreams were starting to unfold before my very eyes. Of course, my response was, "Yes, I would *love* to be your background singer!"

I asked what days the rehearsals were and also mentioned that I didn't drive. I thought this would probably disqualify me but to my surprise she offered to pick me up for rehearsals. I sang with *The Gospelettes* for five years after that and we traveled to many churches in Chicago and around the state.

The manager of the group became a very close friend of mine and we were like God-sisters. She was five years older than me and I learned a great deal from her concerning the music business. In fact, she taught me how to become a booking agent and business manager.

Now, whereas my friend loved the Lord and was always at church, she had a twin sister who was the total opposite of her, and led a questionable lifestyle.

I was still working but not making enough money to continue rent payments on the apartment where I lived alone. One of the ladies that used to sing with *The Gospelettes* told me of a vacancy in her building in Chicago's West Side so I moved upstairs from her, while she lived downstairs. Now I lived close to everyone in the group. My rent was $350 a month and I still had money from my college fund but this was depleting fast.

I started working at a bank as a customer service representative. I was the person that customers called when they needed a check cleared. I loved working at the bank and was there for five years.

Whenever I was finished with my own workload I helped the elderly lady that worked in my department. She was Greek and loved for me to help her. One day she said she was moving back to Greece and that she wanted me to take over her supervisory position. I was very excited about this prospect and started to daydream about it … *If I do get the position of supervisor, I can buy myself nice things, like a house!*

I had not yet taken a vacation that year so I decided to take a week off. When I came back to work, the Greek lady had moved back to Greece and another young lady was working in her place, as the new supervisor! So I went up to the manager and asked why he hadn't given me the supervisory job? He told me that I wasn't qualified. I was the only Black that worked in that department so I started talking to some of my coworkers about what he said. I just wanted to know their opinions relative to my qualifications. That's when they told me about how prejudice the bank was. Three days later I received a telegraph saying that I no longer worked at the bank.

Immediately I went to the unemployment office, showed them the telegram, and filed for unemployment benefits; but the bank tried to fight my claim. All the same, the unemployment office granted me the benefits. After that I moved out of my Chicago West Side apartment because my only source of income now came from unemployment, but it was not enough to sustain me.

Around that same time my good friend, the manager of *The Gospelettes*, got very sick and had to go into the hospital for open-heart surgery. Before the surgery, she had a dream about her late husband who died many years earlier. She dreamed that he came to take her back with him and we joked about it.

On the day of the surgery, I was very nervous and prayed to God that he would heal her. She was released from the hospital six months later ... and then she passed away. The things she taught me about the music business were actually the ground-floor training that launched my future career. She was yet another angel at my side. Right after that, I left *The Gospelettes* and joined another group called *The Tones of Joy,* with whom I sang for the next four years. Knowing that I was looking for work, the manager of *The Tones* offered me a job as a machine operator where he worked during the day, and I was employed there for eight months.

I intended to stay with my cousin and his wife during this time, the ones I babysat for when I was still in college; but, the questionable twin sister of my dear, late friend, happened to be looking for a roommate. Her rent was feasible, she had a house with no furniture and I had furniture with no house, so I decided to move in with her.

Then I got a job working temporarily, got laid off again and ended up on welfare. I made an agreement with the twin that I would pay half the rent with the cash I received from welfare and that all my food stamps would go toward the house. The food stamps were enough for everyone and she agreed. I received $90 cash a month from welfare and $150 for food stamps.

Now, the twin had a son who moved into the house, having just come from the Navy, and what I didn't know was that the two of them liked smoking pot -- lots of it. Every day I smelled the stench of pot invade by bedroom and I was already planning to move out again, but I ended up staying for three years. As the months went by, she and her son started eating up all the food with their friends, because when they smoked pot they got hungry.

One after the other, these adverse situations only served to push me closer to my purpose. I wanted better for myself and was tired of the chaos. I enrolled into another college to enhance my journalism degree because this was my field of choice, so I attended Olive Harvey College, located in Chicago's South Side. Welfare gave me bus tokens to get to and from school. I was finally focused again -- or so I thought.

I started dating a certain guy, and that's when I made the hugest mistake of my life.

There was a guy that I liked at my dad's church. He used to try to talk with me but my affections were engaged elsewhere. At the time I had fallen in love with a certain guy but he wasn't acting right. So, I agreed to meet up with this other guy and we started talking. One night we became intimate and six weeks later I started getting sick.

I went to the doctor and he told me that I was six-and-a-half weeks pregnant. I didn't want to hear that. I was not in love with this guy and I didn't tell him I was pregnant. I kept brushing him off. One day I called home and told my mother that I was pregnant. Right on queue she declared that my baby might be retarded because my sister was also. I was looking for guidance, the help of my mother and yet again, she failed me.

I hung up the phone and start crying and praying. As discussed earlier, whenever my little sister got sick, which was often, she had seizures wherein her body jerked as though struck by lightning. I had to put a spoon in her mouth to prevent her from swallowing her tongue. Leave it up to my mother to put such visions in my head. Those days were rough. My mother didn't give me any guidance so I turned to God, as I always had, for help that I couldn't get from anyone else.

The next day my roommate, the twin, told me she was pregnant also.

Dorean Edwards

She didn't want to keep the baby and was planning to get an abortion. I confessed that I was also pregnant and told her what my mother said about my baby possibly being retarded. Instead of giving me moral support she asked if I wanted to get an abortion as well. She knew of a clinic where the doctor performed abortions for a fee of $200.

With the passing of Roe v. Wade in 1973, abortions were now legal in the United States. I didn't have $200 so I called my aunt to loan it to me until my next paycheck. I was afraid to have a retarded child because I saw what my sister went through and how much attention she required, which I couldn't give my baby at that time. So I got the phone number from my roommate and made the appointment. I was scared and crying at the same time. I didn't tell my family about what I was planning to do, only my mother knew about the pregnancy.

My aunt gave me the money that same day and I went to the doctor. I asked him if the baby was already formed in my womb. He asked if I want to see it on the ultrasound and I declined. I didn't want to remember. Then he gave me a shot and I was taken into the operat-

98

ing room where he performed the procedure. I woke up in the recovery room, which was where they made sure everything was all right following the abortion. I cried in that room wondering if I could physically ever have a child ever again. The doctor told me that my child would have been born on December 8th. Each year I hold that date dear to my heart.

I wanted to leave the twin's house after that but I didn't have the money to move, so I called my dad to borrow it. He said he didn't have any. I asked him to borrow it from someone else on my behalf promising to pay it back, but again he declined. So I made a collect call to my sister. My sister was all grown up by then and married. She had moved to San Diego, California, and studied engineering in the United States Navy. During our conversation she invited me to come and live with her in San Diego. I told her to give me a day to think about this. *Maybe I could find a job there*. I was still grieving from the abortion and, because working was an integral part of my ethic, the stress of not having a job took a heavy toll on me. So I moved to San Diego, California.

Before I left Chicago, some friends of mine gave me a going-away party. They took up a collection, which paid for my one-way ticket to San Diego. My last month in Chicago was spent at my girl-cousin's house. I needed some peace and quiet before traveling and time to grieve. My cousin was so sweet to me. She told me how much she loved me and how much she would miss me. We both shed tears, which really warmed my heart. I asked God to forgive me, to heal my body and allow me to have more children. I told God that I would never abort another child as long as I live. At that moment, the healing of my body and emotions began.

Chapter 16

Gateway to Destiny

The thought of moving to San Diego, California, to live with my sister and her husband soon become exhilarating. I was so looking forward to seeing her again and was equally excited when I boarded the plane. Still struggling now and then with the aftermath of my horrific childhood, I prayed to God that he would keep me focused on positive things, not the negative, and I made a vow to stay true to my ambitions.

As I pondered about what type of work I wanted to apply for, I considered being a youth counselor because I loved working with kids. I always wanted to do something to put a smile on a child's face.

I finally arrived in San Diego and was overjoyed to see my sister. She had a beautiful, little baby in her arms that she was babysitting that day. She asked if I wanted to hold the child and I quickly declined. Flashbacks of my pregnancy and the mental stress I suffered shot through my mind at that moment and holding the baby would only cause me to grieve all over again.

When we arrived at her residence I told her that I was a little exhausted from the plane ride so she showed me to my room. Once in the room I shed tears wondering what my child could had been and what he or she would have looked like. All I had left of my baby was the birthdate of December 8th.

As soon as I got settled in, I went to the welfare office in downtown San Diego and applied for benefits, which they gave me, along with food stamps, a check for spending money, and bus tokens so that I could look for work.

During the ensuing months I started looking for work in the surrounding San Diego areas, starting with the unemployment office. I've always had a strong sense of independence and didn't want to be a burden on my sister. I didn't stay on welfare for very long, because shortly thereafter, I was on my way to the unemployment office again to check the job-board when I saw a young lady handing out flyers and talking to people outside the main entrance. So I walked up to see what she was handing out. She gave me a flyer and said, "This is for people who are interested in going to college in this area." Immediately, I thought, I can do this! So I asked her how much her employers paid her to hand out these flyers and whether they were hiring, and she answered, "Yes, they're hiring at $6 an hour with commissions." That was the pay rate in those days. "You would work six hours a day and get paid for eight."

This sounded like something I could do so I didn't hesitate to ask for her employer's address. That next morning I went to the employer, filled out all the forms and they hired me on the spot! This job afforded me the opportunity to talk, interact and inspire people, which was something that I loved doing, and still do. As promised, I worked only six hours and got paid for eight; a true blessing. Along with the base pay and commissions, God blessed me to make around $1,800 a month! It was now the early 1990s and I was only thirty years old. For that day, this was really good money.

In the meantime, I did miss music in my life. I was musically inclined and often went to Gospel events. I tried to think of ways to stay active in the music ministry, get into a singing group and perform at the local Gospel events but I hadn't found a church yet. So I started asking people all over about a good church to attend in San Diego, and before long they told me about a good one. I started attending a church and met another young man there, just as the church was preparing for service. He and I became good friends and we talked a little on the phone until he left to go back into the service. San Diego is a large Navy and Marine Corp town and boasts the world-famous *Top Gun* fighter jet program, which is a division of the colossal Miramar Naval Air Station. For this reason, service members were coming and going all the time.

I loved meeting and talking to people in the music industry. I met one particular lady at church who told me about a man that sang in a Gospel quartet. I asked if she could have him call me, and he did. He was a well-spoken, very nice gentlemen. He came to pick me up, I met his family and they took me to his Gospel program where his group performed. He introduced me to another, well-known group whom I had actually seen performing in Chicago. I was very excited to see them again and during their performance they tore the house down! In fact, I knew one of the singers and we stopped to talk and reminisce. I had a wonderful time! I'm glad we crossed each other's path because we exchanged phone numbers and promised to stay in touch. We kept that promise and still talk today.

I had now reached the peak of my potential in San Diego and wanted to move to Los Angeles. So I asked the manager at my place of employment if they had any openings in the Los Angeles area that I could transfer to. To my surprise my boss said yes. In fact, they had one opening for a supervisory position. I told him that I'd like to apply for that position.

That night I went home and prayed. I asked God that if this was where he wanted me to go to please give me favor. The next day my manager called me into the office and told me that he took care of everything. I got the supervisory position and they were expecting me on Monday morning! I was so excited! This was the Lord giving back to me what was wrongfully taken by the prejudiced manager at the Chicago bank!

It seemed as though my life had done a total switch from hurt and pain to success and gain. Thank you Jesus, for your many blessings! I went home to tell my sister the good news. I expressed my heartfelt appreciation to her for allowing me to stay in her home for seven months; but it was time for me to leave. She understood and neither of us had any regrets. She was very happy for me and believed in my decision.

That weekend I packed up my suitcase and called my cousin who lived in Los Angeles. I asked if she knew of any vacant apartments that I could rent. She said I didn't need an apartment and that I could stay with her because she had an extra room! She lived in the Los Angeles suburb of Linwood and she wanted me to take my time looking for an apartment instead of rushing into something. This sounded great so I took her up on the offer. That evening I had dinner with my sister and her husband one last time in San Diego and the next morning I caught the Greyhound bus to L.A., whereupon my cousin picked me up at the depot. My cousin's mother was my father's sister. I was happy to finally see L.A. and meet more of my family members. They all had very loving spirits. I was ecstatic about living at my cousin's apartment. She was very sweet and I felt loved as soon as she greeted me. At her apartment I had the opportunity to meet yet another cousin who brought along her children. They were too cute and had freckles just like me. I laughed and thought, *Yep, we're definitely family.*

I told my cousin that I wanted to get into a church and become active in the music ministry, so she invited me to her own church. I attended there several times and ran into a guy who sang with a group that had also performed in Chicago. He had given me his business card back in Chicago and I had kept his card in my file all that time. I was curious to see what might happen with this connection so I called and told him I'd just moved to Los Angeles, and that I would love to come and hear his group perform. He was delighted to hear that I enjoyed his group and agreed to come and pick me up to see his Gospel concert. At the concert the lineup was long and impressive, filled with groups performing all that day. I was excited as I looked around at all the different people, and I thought, *There are good people in this world.* Everyone there was so very nice and I felt like I was finally home in a safe place again.

Monday morning came quickly. I went to my new Los Angeles job and met everyone. I worked at this office for three months, when the company moved to another city that was even closer to my cousin's place, where we lived. I loved my job and tried to exceed their expectations until one day it all paid off. They started giving me bonuses!

In those days, everything was going very well. I was active in church, going to concerts, meeting new friends and enjoying my job. I was no longer trapped in that little girl's body and was now experiencing life to the fullest!

My cousin went home to Arkansas to see her daughter for Christmas and I stayed home at her house. Since I loved cooking, I cooked dinner and invited my sister and her husband from San Diego to come and spend Christmas with me since they lived only two hours away, but she declined and said not this time. So I asked if I could come down there for Christmas but she said they had other plans. So I ended up staying in my cousin's house alone. Times like these really made me think about my mother. Although I missed her, I didn't want to go back there just yet.

Six months had come and gone at my cousin's place in Lynwood, and I was finally ready to get my own place. During the Christmas holidays I walked around Lynwood and came upon a really nice neighborhood. It was a little townhouse community. I saw a townhouse available for rent and fell in love with it immediately. So I told the Lord, "This is the place that I want, Lord." I knocked on the landlord's door and inquired about the rent, which I could afford, so I gave her a down payment. I was so glad that I was in a position to do so. I told her that I would like to move in on my birthday, which was January 22nd.

It was still December and I had a whole month to buy new furniture for the apartment. When my cousin returned from Arkansas I thanked her for allowing me to share a room in her place. It was peaceful in her home and she made me feel very comfortable, but I wanted my own place. I never wanted to be a burden on anyone. I moved on my birthday and when I set foot into my new apartment, I kneeled down and thanked God for blessing me.

I had now been working for the college for five years. I was still avidly going to concerts when a young lady caught my eye at the concert. She was talking with the man that brought me to the concert. He was my God-brother, the same one that was in the Gospel group that performed in Chicago and by then we had become best friends. I walked up and asked her what church she attended, whereupon she invited me to Greater Bethany Community Church, which sounded great!

That Sunday she picked me up with her cute son, about two years of age. As I entered the church, I saw thousands of people in attendance. Everyone there had great hospitality and the ushers in the lobby were very warm as they greeted everyone with a smile. So I sat down to hear the preacher who was extremely eloquent.

He spoke relevant things into my spirit and it was evident that God was speaking to me through him. God led me there and I joined the church officially, that same day.

After the service, I went toward the back of the church and filled out the membership form. However, the form featured another pastor's name on it so I asked the minister standing there who he was. It was the senior pastor of the church. So I inquired who the speaker was that morning. He replied *Bishop Noel Jones.*

I told the minister that I wanted to go to *his* church, to which he replied that I'd have to move to Texas because that's where he's from. This angered me and I thought, *Wow! I got tricked into joining this church! I don't know whether I want to keep coming here or not.* I just wanted to hear the senior pastor of this church speak first, before I joined. It turns out that the senior pastor was also an excellent, inspiring speaker. His anointing was the same, his message spoke relevant things to my spirit, and so I stayed.

Meantime, I asked when *Noel Jones* would return because I really enjoyed his ministry. The minister replied that he would be back the following January. I couldn't wait to see him again; he was just that anointed! The result was, I finally found a church that I could call home. I felt a great peace in my spirit as this was the place where God wanted me to be. Things were off to a great start in my new, independent life in L.A.

Then one day my place of employment called to inform me that they were planning to file bankruptcy in the near future, which meant the end of my beloved job. I was devastated and started saving my money. I received this news just when things took a positive turn in my life. They told me not to worry about it right now, but in seven months they would be bankrupt and closed their doors for business.

I started going on a fast because I didn't want to live with anyone else. I enjoyed living on my own, so I became proactive and filled out job applications early. No one was hiring at that time for my type of work and money was getting low. I prayed to God for his help, knowing he didn't bring me this far, and place me in a church where I felt his peace, only to leave me now.

I was led to fill out an application for a customer service, supervisory position in the nearby mall. It came through and I began working there. I was with the company for three years. Then this company started talking about moving away to Texas and that's when my tormented mind re-emerged. *Really? Again Lord? Why are my jobs always moving out of town or going bankrupt? What are you trying to tell me, Lord?* Little did I know, this was the gateway to my destiny -- but the devil wasn't done with me just yet.

Chapter 17

Steal, Kill, Destroy

While working at the mall, my church was selling BBQ dinners one Friday and Saturday to raise money and I told my co-workers about it. In turn, they wanted BBQ dinners delivered to our office. So I called the church and asked them to deliver the dinners; they agreed and I ended up selling $400 worth of dinners!

I came home, put the money in an envelope and placed it in my Bible. I called the people at my church to let them know I had received $400 for the dinners, whereupon they instructed me to bring the money in on Sunday. I also had $1,500 worth of money orders in my apartment to pay bills but I had not yet written them out. So I put the money orders on the dresser and was planning to pay my bills the following day. It was getting late that night so I went to my bedroom and prepared myself for bed. I looked at the clock, it was 1:00 A.M., and then I fell asleep.

A little while later something woke me up! Someone had just entered my bedroom and pressed a cold pistol against my head! Suddenly two men stood at my bed. They tied a cloth around my eyes, and said if I screamed they would blow my head off.

I was terrified and started praying out loud. They told me again to shut up or they'd blow my head off, so I prayed in silence. My mind flashed back to Chicago then. Two men with a knife pressed against my throat, blind-folded me, dragged me into an alley and robbed me. I thought I was going to die but God spared my life again. My attention returned to the men now standing in my bedroom. *What if they kill me? They could kill me and no one would ever know that I'm dead.* They asked for all my money, rummaged through my dresser and saw the money orders. Then they asked if I had any more money. Shaking, scared and praying, I said no. I had actually forgotten about the BBQ cash hidden in my Bible.

Then they tore off my clothes and raped me. I prayed and cried in silence. Then I remembered the promise of the Lord. *No weapon formed against me shall prosper.* I was crying this in my mind and quoting Psalms 91 at the same time as they raped me.

Then my phone rang. Suddenly, they jumped off me and left. They stole my money orders, my television and stereo. I was in shock. I jumped up in tears and ran to the door to double lock it. Then I called the police and my cousin. My cousin came right over and gave me a big hug. She told me not to worry because God had my back. She also prayed with me.

The police took a report and said I needed to go to the hospital, so I got dressed and went to the emergency room. They checked my body to see if I had caught any sexually tranomitted diseases from those guys and, thank God, I hadn't. All the tests came back negative. When I got home I took a good, long, hot shower and washed my body over and over.

That night the devil came to steal, kill and destroy, because God's destiny for me was about to be revealed.

I called my mother but she didn't answer her phone, so I left a message. I called her again and she still didn't answer the phone. I called her between 2:30 in the morning until 7:00 A.M. I kept saying to myself, *I need to talk to my mom! Why won't she return my call?* Then I just gave up; I just kept crying. I called my brothers and told them what had happened and they all said they'd fly to Los Angeles to see me. They told me not to worry and that they would keep me in their prayers. But I still wanted to hear from my mother. I just wanted that motherly comfort.

The next day was Sunday and the church bus came to pick me up. I politely told the bus drive what had happened to me and he said he'd tell the church about it. I gave him the $400 for the church BBQs that were hidden in my Bible. I was functioning on the outside but within myself I contemplated suicide. I made preparations to take an overdose of pills. I just couldn't go on.

Later on that day some of the church members came by to pray and check on me. They also gave me some money. I was now further convinced this church was the right one for me. I stayed at the church and have been a member there or twenty-six years.

As the months went by, I was again on my way to a total healing. The Lord healed me from that tragedy through the love and care of the church members. The day after the rape, my mother finally called at eight o'clock at night. I was very frustrated about her not calling me sooner and I really didn't want to speak to her. I did tell her what happened and all she said was that she was sorry this happened to me, and that she would be praying for me. But that wasn't good enough. I wanted her to tell me she'd be on her way to stay with me for a week or two; but she didn't.

I invited her to come and visit for Christmas and she declined; something about, she wanted to be home with her grand-kids. So I invited her to come and see me on Mother's Day and she again declined. Then I invited her to come for her birthday and that's when she finally agreed. We actually had a wonderful time!

In fact, I went to visit my mother every two years after that and we became best friends until she went home to be with the Lord at the age of seventy-three.

During our time together my mother brought up our past when I was growing up. She actually expressed how sorry she was for everything she had ever done. Before she died she also apologized for not protecting me against the man she married. She also said she loved me and asked me to forgive her. I did so and took her to church with me in Los Angeles. I believe my mother is now with the Lord. Maybe society cannot understand how I could forgive all those people that hurt me. But then think about what we've all done. If God held a grudge, we'd all be dead. He without sin should cast the first stone. In any case, my destiny was about to be revealed, and that's why the devil had attacked me one last time.

Chapter 18

My Destiny Explosion

After my job ended at the college I again found myself seeking employment and I landed a job at the May Company in the Refund Department. After three years -- wait for it, here it comes -- the department moved to Texas, whereupon I found myself out of work once again.

Then a door opened for me that I barely recognized as the opportunity of a life-time. A friend of mine told me about an opening at a record store. *What? I don't want to work at a record store?!* I didn't want it but it was a job, just until I found what I was *really* looking for. Unbeknownst to me, the whole thing was a set-up by the Lord. It was the gateway to my destiny explosion.

I met with the store owner and manager who were actually very nice people. During our meeting I learned that they often conducted autograph-signings for well-known artists, right there at the store! Now that got my attention. The Lord was going to drop industry connections *right into my lap.* So I accepted the job and worked at the store over the next three years.

One day I was riding the bus to work and someone gave me a flyer about an up-coming concert. The flyer featured the entire list of Gospel artists who had won *Grammies* and *Stellar Awards!* The contact name on the flyer was *Frank Badami.* Immediately, I said to myself, *Lord I would love to work with this man on his concerts.* When I arrived at work, I opened up the record store and called the number on the flyer.

Frank Badami and I spoke for a while on the telephone, whereupon he came into the store shortly thereafter. Frank was, and still is, a well-known Los Angeles Gospel music video producer, television producer and concert promoter. When he walked in I felt an immediate connection with him and he hired me to work for him! Over the next three years, Frank called upon me to help him with concert promotions, whereupon I was exposed to many other promotional opportunities, while continuing to work at the store. Concert promotion seemed to be just the thing for me and I began to search for additional opportunities. Before long, I met many other concert promoters and assisted them as well. Naturally, I accumulated an extensive list of celebrity connections. As a result, my name began to circulate and I became well-known around the Gospel music community, in Los Angeles and beyond.

However, my insatiable appetite for music and media didn't stop there. I started working part-time as a freelance writer for *Gospel USA Magazine* and I interviewed artists like *Shirley Caesar, Mighty Clouds of Joy, The Winans* and *Yolanda Adams*, just to name a few. Just as I had envisioned when I was a young, college girl, I was now interviewing celebrities!

My early beginnings at the record store led to many long-lasting friendships. For instance, today I am the publicist for *Grammy Legend Gerald Alston*, lead singer of *The Manhattans*.

Gerald Alston recently produced his first Gospel album featuring four-time, *Grammy* and *Stellar Award Winners, Regina Belle* and *Will Downing, Jr.* Back in the

1980s Gerald was one of my favorite artists and today we are the best of friends.

Now, the annual *Stellar Awards* came up in Los Angeles and I went there to interview the artists and celebrities on behalf of *Gospel USA Magazine*. At the event I observed a lovely woman coordinating all the groups, choirs and solo artists. She seemed like the person in charge, so I walked over to her and politely asked what her position was at the *Stellar Awards*. She replied that she was the producer of the show, which she still is.

Barbara Wilson was approachable, very nice and humble. I said to myself, *I would really like to do what's she's doing!* We became fast friends and still are today. She is my mentor and yet another guardian angel at my side. Barbara and I spoke many times about my mother and she always managed to find ways to encourage me -- she has that gift! She never said anything negative about my mother. She just encouraged me to forgive, let go and let God. I truly thank God for sending such a positive influence into my life. Eventually, Barbara asked me to serve as the *Chairperson of the Stellar Awards' Ballot*, and I handled that function for one year. Barbara enabled me to activate some gifts that God had given me; in particular, working with talent directly, which was a skill that I would soon need.

About this time, our precious pastor at church regretfully passed away. While our congregation was heartbroken, something wonderful happened. *Bishop Noel Jones* moved from Texas to Los Angeles and became our new pastor! He would soon prove to be yet another angel at my side.

Bishop Jones, like me, was a great music lover. After he got settled into our church, he began to schedule music artists to perform at our banquets and fund-raisers. One Sunday, I needed to hear a definite word from the Lord and it came just in time. *Bishop Jones*, preached an anointed sermon that day, which seemed directed right at me, entitled, *For Love Alone*. It was Part 1 of a two-part series. The sermons spoke about love; something that I didn't understand. Those two sermons blessed my soul beyond measure. I felt so freed and fed by these messages that I felt compelled to walk up to the bishop after the service and I said, "Thank you for blessing my soul!"

That's when his security detail told him, "This is Dorean Edwards. She works with celebrities."

By then I was involved with major concert promoters all over Southern California and his security personnel had often seen me working with the celebrities. The bishop took note of this, thanked me for the kind words and then asked for my phone number because he wanted me to start booking Gospel talent for our church. He also gave me his number, for me to call him. I was really nervous about this and thankful at the same time.

Having now acquired the necessary connections and skills I became the bishop's talent coordinator, whereupon I booked such Gospel music greats as, the late-great *Andrea Crouch, Cece Winans, Donnie McClurkin, Fred Hammond, Kirk Whalum, George Duke, Karen Clark Sheard, Kim Burrell* and *Marvin Sapp*, just to name few. I also helped promote a concert in Los Angeles for *Kirk Franklin*. And I did quite well putting these events together.

I was still working at the record store during this time when *Bishop Jones* asked me to book yet another group – *The Williams Brothers*. So I contacted the group and began to promote the event. The store manager and I coordinated the autograph-signing for the *Williams*

Brothers and we sold tickets to the event at the store, and at church.

On the day of the signing, two young ladies walked in. They were sisters who knew the *Williams Brothers*. While talking with them, they happened to mention that their mother was not well. She could not stand in line for too long but would love to attend the concert. So I promised the girls that I would reserve a good seat for their mother, free of charge. The girls' mother attended the concert with her grandchildren, which made the lady very happy.

This connection proved to be the most astounding of all, as you'll soon see.

I had now been working at the record store for three years and I began to feel restless. So I started looking for larger media opportunities. I landed a position at a Los Angeles radio station, where I worked as a promoter. I handled advertising, promotions and interviews. I also recruited new, record-label artists and connected them with different radio stations; an invaluable service for the new artists. I was doing quite well for a long time while, when one day, the radio station called me into the office to announce that the company was moving to

San Diego. The new radio station there was to be a 24-hour Gospel radio program. They asked if I wanted to transfer with them but I declined.

So now I found myself looking for work and I again fell into despair. It became very apparent to me that I would soon have to start up my own company, to shelter me from all these lay-offs.

Now, let's recall the two sisters whose mother I had seated at *The Williams Brothers'* concert. We had become great friends at the time so I told them that I was once again looking for work. Well, it just so happened that one of the sisters had her own fundraising company and she been working with *Stevie Wonder* on fundraisers for years! She ended up hiring me as an assistant to help with the events.

That year, *Bishop Noel Jones'* birthday was coming up and I asked the Lord to help me do something so wonderful for him, that he would never forget it. And then I had an idea. I asked my new boss, if she would ask *Stevie Wonder* to come to our church and sing at *Bishop Jones'* birthday celebration. She promised to ask Stevie if he would consider doing it, and I heard no more about it after that. In fact, I never mentioned it to the bishop, as this was to be a birthday surprise. On the morning of the bishop's celebration, I went into the prayer room and asked the Lord to bring *Stevie Wonder* to the church. I also told a few people that I was believing the Lord to bring him and of course, they replied, "What? Stevie Wonder? That's never gonna' happen!"

The praise and worship service had just ended as the bishop was seated on the stage, getting ready to deliver his message. Then a friend of mine leaned over to me and said, "Stevie Wonder's not gonna's come here!" Just then, I looked up the isle ...

And here comes Stevie Wonder!

His assistant helped him onto the stage whereupon *Bishop Noel Jones*, the great lover of music, beamed a smile that I'll never forget. As soon as they recognized *Stevie Wonder*, the entire congregation sprang to their feet and exploded with a roar of cheers and applause!

And then, *Stevie Wonder*, the winner of twenty-five *Grammy Awards*, and *1996 Grammy Lifetime Achievement Award Winner*, assumed his position at the piano and delivered his golden gift. His birthday gift to *Bishop Noel Jones* was sublime; a thing of supernatural beauty!

~ ~ ~ ~ ~ ~

So much for the nay-sayers. I thank the Lord for placing me in a position to facilitate the bishop's birthday gift.

> Now that God had strategically positioned me with a literal gold-mine of influential connections, he broke open my **Seal of Destiny** and unleashed the work he called me to do.

One day I was watching the news when they ran a special report about a boy who walked into a school with a gun. The security video showed the boy shooting at people. Therefore, I contemplated ways to bring about positive changes into the lives of our youth. I prayed and sought guidance from the Lord to give me direction – and he did so.

I woke up the next morning, made a call to *Bishop Jones* and asked if I could produce a Gospel youth seminar. I told him, "I want to brand the conference as the *Stop the Violence, Think Education, Put God First, Concert & Conference.* The theme of the conference would be *Youth Empowerment 4 Destiny.*"

Bishop Jones agreed and I started calling youth pastors and leaders all over the city about my vision and they all partnered up with me. My first youth event was a complete success!

The first celebrity guests to participate were actors *Chris Tucker* and *Larenz Tate.* Chris had a new movie out called *Rush Hour* and *Larenz Tate's* movie, *Why Do Fools Fall in Love,* had also just been released. *Larenz* played the late-great *Frankie Lymon* in the film.

The success of this event was staggering! The house was packed with youth from other churches all around. I was extremely elated about its success. I knew God had blessed it, and I praised him for it. My purpose in life was finally revealed and I was thankful that I made the decision to stay alive to see it materialize.

Ever since then, I've been doing my *Back-2-School Conferences* and other productions for God, focusing toward the inner-city youth. We are on our sixteenth year of celebrating our youth.

The creativity that God blessed me with continued to unfold to even greater levels and further outreach opportunities that I never dreamed of. No wonder the devil wanted to kill me!

Then I put together a workshop with a well-known fashion designer to come and talk to the youth about becoming entrepreneurs and making clothes for celebrities. Kids love fashion and this was a youth-only event. Kids love music too. So I also created a youth music workshop, and had a well-known music producer come in and talk with the kids about becoming a music producer. He brought in all his equipment and had the kids participate in writing a song that day. All the conferences and workshops were geared towards educating and preparing kids for the real world. The kids loved these events! Our youth workshops also offered Computer Analysis classes. We brought in computers and laptops for the kids and free give-a-ways. With these devices, the kids experienced the world-wide-web and networking perhaps for the first time. I made sure to give them lots of educational things that would benefit them in their daily lives and futures!

I also implemented a workshop for young entrepreneurs, starting at the age of seven, which entailed a youth-panel discussion, plus question and answer sessions afterward. This gave the youth an opportunity to express themselves by asking questions about various industries, to people who actually worked in them. We closed out the conference with the *Hour of Power Hip Hop Concert*.

The events started at 9:00 A.M. and ran until 9:00 P.M. We fed over three-thousand inner-city youth every year immediately after the events. We also provided them with professional grooming services performed by volunteers who cut and braided their hair. Then we gave the kids three thousand back-to-school supplies, clothing, uniforms, and tennis shoes.

To close out the celebration we rolled out the *Star-Studded Red Carpet Event* from 6:00 P.M. to 9:00 P.M., at which time celebrities and performing artists came out and socialized with the youth on behalf of my company, *Consultant Entertainment*.

Among the celebrities hosting these evening events were: *Tia & Tamera, Tahj Mowery, Chris Tucker, Larenz Tate, The Rapper Game, Tichina Arnold* from the *Martin Lawrence Show*, TV producer *Bill Duke*, the cast of *The Bernie Mac Show: Meagan Good, Hill Harper, Trey Smith (son of Will Smith)*, and *Carlon Jeffrey*, who played *Cameron Parks* on the *Disney Channel*, and *Carlos Knight* from *Super Ninja* on *Nickelodeon*, plus *Flex Alexander, Nick*

Cannon, and *Kel Mitchell* from the *Kenan & Kel Show* on *Nickelodeon,* just to name a few. God blessed me to work with wonderful artists over the years and I give him all the glory.

Bishop Noel Jones was a guardian angel sent to my side, as was the lady on the bus so long ago, as well as the manager of *The Gospelettes,* who took me under her wing. Later in life came my great friend, *Barbara Wilson,* producer of the *Stellar Awards,* and *Frank Badami,* the Los Angeles concert promoter; all of whom were angels sent by God into my life.

As my destiny exploded before my eyes over the years, my heart overflowed with a new contentment. Seeing all that the Lord had done in my life, put a smile on my face every day, and it made the devil hate me even more. He knew perfectly well that he had lost the fight. He knew that the Lord's favor was upon me and that I would be working with the youth. Satan is possessively jealous of the youth generation because they are the easiest to influence. If he can put his hooks into them early in life, he can make them do anything he wants later in life.

The programs that the Lord propelled me to initiate took our youth and set their feet in a new, sturdy, dignified direction with life-long results.

I stayed focused and learned how to forgive all those people who hurt me in the past. I would not allow anyone or anything to stand in my way of success! As a result, God turned my pain into my passion. I pray that this roadmap of stubborn, never-give-up conviction will prove to you that your destiny can transcend your pain and suffering and lead you straight to your heart's desire. Forgiveness never goes unrewarded.

I'm free to work the visions that God blessed me to do. I'm no longer trapped in that little girl's body. This woman is free to come out and be in a position to help others by telling her story. Once I was a little, abused, neglected and unprotected little girl, in great need of healing, and the Lord made sure to send me the right people at the right time. You too can be set free! My hope is that you will come out of hiding, forgive those that wronged you and be healed!

God has a purpose for you!

Today, I'm the corporate CEO of *Consultant Entertainment*. The Lord raised me up to be a successful, Gospel music entertainment specialist, with over twenty-five years' experience, promoting recording artists and positive entertainment projects. My events are being talked about all over the world.

Whereas the devil tried to kill me, it didn't work.

I'm still here.

I win!

Acknowledgements

I would like to give special thanks to the following people, all of whom play amazing roles in my life:

Carole Cobb; my good friend, who is sent by God and has always been a blessing to me---and still is.

Barbara Wilson; my mentor, dear friend and producer of the *Stellar Awards*. Words cannot express my gratitude! I don't know what I would do without the wisdom and knowledge you imparted in me. I thank God for allowing you to be an influential part of my life! Since the day I met you, I have always treasured your sisterhood and will be forever grateful for our friendship.

Delaina Stewart; my good friend, for helping me to put the account of my life into words. You are such a positive influence in my life. I thank God for your creativity and the gift He has given you for words. You are truly God-sent and I will always cherish you like a sister. Thank you for you sacrifice and helping me to finish this book. I know it was God who inspired you through countless, tireless nights to assist and motivate me. I now understand the meaning of Philippians 1:6 -- *He who began a good work in you, will complete it until the day of Jesus Christ.* I am forever thankful.

Willett Duvall; how do I find the words to say how thankful I am for your continuous support?. You are a woman that has always been there from the beginning to the end of my projects. I praise God for you and know that you too are God-sent.

Janice Lewis; my dear friend, you seem to always step in and offer advice or help when I'm stuck on a project. Whether it's funding, assisting or motivating, you have always been there for me. Your consistency gives true meaning to friendship, and I do so appreciate you.

Herman Williams; thank you for lending me your ear as I read and reread the chapters of my book. I thank you for listening repeatedly; my love for you is that of a brother.

Dominique Lawrence Thomas and your family; what can I say, besides thank you for always praying and interceding for me and encouraging me along the way. I thank you for be there for me. I don't take this for granted.

Pamela Broussard; last but not least -- my good, long-time friend, you're the angel whom God strategically placed in my life. You've helped me in so many ways. I will always cherish and respect your friendship. I can say with confidence that you are like a sister to me and I thank Him for our friendship.

And to my dear late friend, the manager of The Gospelettes, who gave me my early start in the entertainment industry.

I also want to thank my first best friend, Debra Ligon, whom God sent into my life when I first came to Los Angeles thirty years ago. Much love to you, Debra! We're still best friends to this day!

To all my God-sisters and God-brothers, and everyone else God placed in my life I truly appreciate you all. Most of all, I thank God for my family and loved ones. May God continually bless you all.

I'd like to express my gratitude and sincere love. Words cannot express how much I appreciate you for contributing to my life. It's because of people like you that I am no longer *Trapped in A Little Girl's Body*. Each time you cross my mind, I find myself smiling with a glad heart.

I will always appreciate, respect and value our friendship.

Love, peace and blessings to you all,

Dorean Edwards

Meet the Author

Dorean Edwards is the founder and corporate CEO of *Consultant Entertainment*, a Los Angeles based production firm, specializing in music concerts, youth events and educational workshops focused on inner-city youth. She is best known for launching the wildly successful, *Stop the Violence, Think Education, Put God First, Concert & Conference* events, as well as the *Youth Empowerment 4 Destiny* workshops, which connects A-list Hollywood celebrities to youths, ages 7 to 18. She resides in Los Angeles with her extended family and continues her much-publicized work for Christ, with no end in sight.

Contact Information

To contact Ms. Edwards regarding speaking engagements, order more copies of this book or general correspondence, please write:

Consultant Entertainment Media
Dorean Edwards
Email: edwardsdorean@yahoo.com

To view Ms. Edwards and her clients
Visit her on Facebook:
https://www.facebook.com/edwardsdorean

Then follow her on Twitter!
@doreanedwards

If you'd like to meet Ms. Edwards
in person, visit:

West Angeles Church of God in Christ
With Bishop Charles E. Blake
3600 W. Crenshaw Blvd.
Los Angeles California, 90016

Made in the USA
San Bernardino, CA
13 March 2019